STOP! DON'T READ THIS

# STOP! DON'T READ THIS

## *the story*

*Leonora Rustamova*

Copyright © Leonora Rustamova 2011

First published in 2011 by
Bluemoose Books Ltd
25 Sackville Street
Hebden Bridge
West Yorkshire
HX7 7DJ

www.bluemoosebooks.com

British Library Cataloguing-in-Publication data
A catalogue record for this book is available from the-British-Library

Paperback  ISBN 13: 978-0-956687630

Printed and bound in the UK by Henry Ling Ltd, Dorchester

# About the Author

Leonora Rustamova lives in her native Yorkshire with her sixteen year-old daughter, Flora. She was a passionate and popular teacher for more than ten years, and then she wrote a story that got her sacked, or was she really saved? Read her own telling of what happened, her thoughts and insights into teaching, teenagers and more, and of course you can make up your own mind about THAT story.

# Author's Note

**This book is a memoir enfolding a fictional story written for and in the idiom of six real people. If you still have your youth and something better to do than reading all the boring mouldy grown up bits you can skip ahead about fifteen pages to the beginning of the real story, and miss out the italics altogether.**

The school we all attended was described at that time by the schools' inspectorate as a good school with some excellent features; it had a hard-working and committed staff, and could have been any state school of our times, anywhere. The problems and behaviours of the students are based on current national issues facing many teenagers and the staff who teach them. We feel our story is important nationally and not in the incidental context of one particular school. We form a partnership in production of this book.

The school staff in the story are all invented, except Mr Blero and Mr Carson who are based on my friends Steve Cann and Gavin Mulholland. Conversations with the Commy Boys between chapters are not factual, but are representative of our interactions.

The original story was written purely to encourage teenagers to read and is not written in conventional book style. Reading is important, and I think it's worth ignoring a lot of formal language use and punctuation to make that easier at the start. The language is idiomatic, so don't be upset by the generous usage of words like 'like', and if there is an acronym or a word that you don't understand as an adult- please don't assume it is a typo, ask a child to tell you what it means! We adults love to show off and impart our knowledge to young people, and they love a chance to do the same to us.

All sections which have a chapter heading, and the epilogue, comprise the original story 'STOP! Don't read this!' (copyright Leonora Rustamova 2008), and other real documents referred to are referenced. The dialogue between myself and a former student copied verbatim from a chatbox is anonymised at his request. He shall remain The Unknown Soldier, representing as he does, many young people who have not found their rightful place in our education system. The description of the disciplinary process is taken from documents which are no longer confidential. The rest is based on my personal thoughts and experiences in eleven years of teaching, a job which is not for the work-shy or the faint-hearted, and which is getting harder for its practitioners day by day.

*Leonora Rustamova*

*A novel is a mirror, carried along a main road.*

*Stendhal*
*1783–1842*

For the Commy Boys: Greg, Christie,
Travis, Billy and Martin.

For Jago, who was with us all the way.

And for my daughter, Flora, who had to be
the mum when times got hard.

*If I am going to try and explain this story to you, I should probably start in the car park, on the 19th January, where I stood, staring back at my school, thinking "Fuck. Fuck. Fuck!"*

*I was trying to get my head round what had just happened: one minute I was stepping up for Monday morning period one, and the next minute I was heading home, suspended. I got escorted to the gate, under strict instructions not to speak to anybody. I wouldn't mind, but I actually love school, and I've always rather fancied myself as a bit of a swot. It's true there had been a lot of rant at smokers' corner about The Dark Side getting a grip of the place, but I've worked in education for years, so I've long since accepted that as the standard topic at any smokers' corner where teachers form the group. It doesn't necessarily mean the Dark Side are getting a grip, does it. Dark Side or not, it seems a little excessive to go from Number One Swot to Villain Number One in a five minute interview. But that is basically what happened. There was a letter on the mat when I got home congratulating me on my recent promotion. It was closely followed by another confirming my suspension. Both the promotion and the suspension were for the same thing: a commitment to pulling in marginalised kids. The lunacy of this contradiction has actually helped keep me sane, along with the kids themselves who wouldn't let me disappear when I found myself on the margin.*

*I like those back-to-the-future movies like Terminator where time goes in a circle. Where the past happens because of the future and the future happens because of the past. Like they send some guy in a time-machine back to 1756 or whatever, and he has to kill a couple of armies, and survive a tsunami, just to move a piece of wood or something two inches to the left; so that time machines will be invented in the future, so some guy can go back in one, to move the piece of wood again. It all loops round and you can't find the beginning or the end. It's like if you got a chicken and an egg and somehow fused them together and they formed a hoop and you spun it.*

*When life gets complicated, you find yourself thinking over and over the same things. Round and round you go. Maybe that is the brain's way of saying that it's sometimes easier to work out what's happening if you see Time as a circle. It gives you more of a chance to spot the patterns. I worked as a teacher in one school for 11 years. I loved every brick of the mouldy old place. It was my mission on Earth. It taught me a lot about who I am, my strengths and my weaknesses, and then it shoved me out into the wide world and closed the door. Still, I suppose that is what schools generally do to kids one way or another.*

*Someone once said life gives you the same lesson over and over again until you learn it. Which is really why I am now writing this book; after getting kicked out of school, and being internationally disgraced, for writing this book.*

*Funny old world.*

# A Brief History of the Commy Boys

The adoption of a programme in our school called The Construction Academy was catalysed by a perceived need to provide some sort of useful education for a group of boys who, even as young as twelve, were pretty unteachable en masse. It was clear that these boys were going to present an increasing problem. Most were simply regarded as non-academic and practical skills were deemed to be more useful for them to acquire. Thus they became The Commy Boys, a name they gave themselves as a short form of Construction Academy. By their fourth year of school they were infamous; staff were carefully selected to teach them and had to agree to do it in advance.

School saw fit to try and get exam grades for these students a year early as it looked unlikely that it would be tenable to keep them on in their final year. The group were expected to be out on bricklaying and joinery courses from Monday till Wednesday, and to come in for some core subjects: English, Maths, Technology and IT on Thursday and Friday. Due to the various issues of behaviour and need this didn't hold up neatly for very long. They were already damaged in their attitude towards authority for many reasons and as placements broke down, holes developed in their week where they had no provision at all.

One spent many of the winter Mondays in bed because he had no course to go to. As I have discovered myself since losing my job, when you live in an underfunded home, the school day has practical attractions we often forget, not least of which is heating. Wednesday mornings became another time when they had no timetabled lessons and were often wandering the building waiting for their day to start after break.

Of course school tried to sort out some useful occupation for them but it isn't easy once the year has started and everyone is already committed. They were not the kind of group that people could absorb easily into other areas by that point. They spent some time in Technology but caused quite a bit of menace to other students already timetabled into those classes, and removed a few items of equipment. Often the boys would sit in the dining room feeling resentful towards anyone who passed. Staff were generally uncomfortable with confronting them. Their exclusions, detentions, truancy, dubious social skills and police contact were heading for exponential by the end of the autumn term.

This is not to say that strategies weren't being tried. Senior Staff were tirelessly rounding them up and returning them to classrooms. The headteacher mentored one of them personally. Placements were approached, learning from home was implemented and they were encouraged in sport. The Commy Boys got wilder. There were fights in and out of lessons. They were abusive to staff and the general public. They were in a shocking state and their presence was intimidating in school. I'm not saying they didn't have their reasons.

Because they were so wild, people resorted to detentions and exclusions before they managed to establish any kind of a relationship with these students, to the point where it was extremely unlikely they would make it to the end of the year. To achieve any successful transition to the next step in life after school, making it to the official leavers' date is crucial. Teachers know this and use it as a threat and an encouragement to students to modify their attitudes. Students, as many of us adults know too well, do not always understand this fully until it is too late. It is one of those things that cause teachers and parents to bang their heads against the brick wall of teenagers at some time or another.

The CA was set up for good reasons and is a valuable part of school provision. It was just unfortunate that some of the boys in the cohort were put into it for emotional/behavioural reasons and not for their true academic needs. This is the kind of thing that happens to these sorts of lads all over the country. The reason for this is simple. By the time they get to us, they are already hard to reach and they get harder and harder to reach as they proceed through adolescence in a large and busy school where time and resources are limited. They can't trust you to stick by them when things get difficult, and things got difficult very quickly around the Commy Boys.

I was asked to take half of the group for the final year of their course. They were well on the road to educational rack and ruin by then. One was said to be unable to read at all. They were described as overtly racist, violent and misogynistic in their presentation in school and the wider community at that time. I was told – they are a pack, and they hunt you like a pack. I agreed to take them on.

My first encounter with them prior to our English lessons was in the corridor in July. They kind of swirled out of the crowd and came to a halt in front of me. Greg said,

"We've got you for English in September and we're gonna break you!"

It would be funny how totally prophetic that turned out to be given my current situation, if it wasn't for the fact that it is not

5

funny at all, but you can't make an omelette without breaking the eggs as they say.

On the way into our first class, they sprayed Lynx on their arms, and lit it, giving a kind of apocalyptic symbolism to the start of the year. They went on to explain defiantly that they had done their English GCSE the previous year because school had hoped to come up with a way of getting rid of them all by now but hadn't managed to find anyone who would take them. I was saddened (and dare I say it just a little bit impressed) at this analysis of their predicament and was determined to improve their feelings towards school. I don't remember managing to get them to sit down at all, but I did succeed in getting custody of the lighter when one of them aimed the Lynx can at the crotch of his schoolpants. I appreciate a bit of dramatic significance as much as the next person; however, the flaming groin region of a teenage boy is something most definitely to be avoided at all costs.

School wanted rid of these boys really, just as they had inferred. The system couldn't deal with them effectively because they felt they were outside the system. In that first lesson alone, there were countless punishable offences, and yet a punishment is only useful as a marker for going beyond a boundary – they were all beyond that before they got through the door. Education should be able to do something creative for the desperate few. They don't come along very often after all, and every child should matter. Something was needed to improve their attitudes, to help them on their way to the next stage. I wanted to show them sympathy, try to be patient while I came up with a valid plan, but of course they were used to new hands offering them understanding and then getting desperate and falling back on sanctions. I think they wanted to get it out of the way as quickly as possible, to show they weren't fooled by the friendly approach of authority any more. It's not surprising how little time it takes a teacher to get aggressive with a group like that. They were bewildering, and bewilderment is not a comfortable feeling when you are meant to be in charge.

A few lessons in to the year and we were writing lists of adjectives to describe favourite things. This was going well; everyone was sitting down, everyone was more or less writing answers and I was feeling rather pleased. We'd discussed favourite cars and put their characteristics on paper. Favourite colour was the next subject for description, safe enough I thought, until one of them shouted out, "I know what my favourite colour is Miss. It's the colour of your cunt." Just like that. While I was still stunned he followed it up with, "I was thinking about it last night". I had never experienced anything like that level of challenge from a student in all my years of teaching. Nothing even anywhere close. I had to fight the desire to have this boy removed permanently and make myself appreciate the kind of tests severely disaffected students run on you to see whether you will quit when it gets tough. I still hadn't issued a single punishment by that point and it is important not to lose your advantage with a class you are going to teach all year. I would have certainly had no way back with this boy if I had responded to his shocking attack. The fact that I let it go was all he needed to become an ally. He knew I could have had him out for that and I think he honoured the fact that I swallowed my pride to keep our relationship. I told him that when he knew me better he would feel bad about saying that, and I was prepared to wait. As it turned out I didn't have to wait long after that. He began volunteering to read aloud to the rest of the group. I was grateful for this because they all had to shut up when Billy was reading. He held more sway with the group than I did.

Our relationship gradually improved. I bought them hot chocolate because they had to sit still to drink it and because, to be perfectly honest they were badly in need of a bit of sweetness. They felt like they didn't matter to the school and I wanted them to feel that they did. The Commy Boys were exceptional in many ways. I found they had emotional preoccupations with all kinds of serious things. They were out of school working with 'blokes' more than half the week and felt older and somewhat marginalised from their year group. They had very keen brains on the wrong trajectory. Between them they had already had the kind of collection of life experiences that in ways made them older than me. Some of their experiences are beyond my worst nightmares.

The most exceptional thing about them for me was their morality. It inspired me to get to know them better and I can best explain it with reference to Kohlberg's definitive research into stages of moral judgement. When I first met the Commy Boys, they could have been argued to fit into the category defined as 'Preconventional Morality'. This registers around Stage 1 in Kohlberg's table and is normally reserved for very young children: no sense of value for following codes of conduct, no empathy for other people's positions, no respect for other people's personal property and so on. Within their own isolated group however, I'd say they were touching Stage 6, and Stage 6 is a rare one to get to. Kohlberg found that many adults rarely achieve this stage – characterised by formulating abstract ethical principles and upholding them to avoid self-condemnation. He points out that children are 'moral philosophers' who develop moral standards of their own. These standards do not necessarily come from peers or parents, rather they emerge from the cognitive interaction of children with their social environment.

The complex, marginalised and fiercely loyal code of the Commy Boys made them stick together and resist interaction with authority in school despite the fact that they didn't necessarily all like each other. They had an inviolable and sophisticated moral code which existed strictly between themselves, and which accounted for each other's personal failings with a quite devastating acknowledgement of their own individual realities. They shared their spoils, they stuck by each other, and they knew how far to trust each other in an array of situations. If you can show kids you've spotted their qualities, you can deal with how they use them and expand them out later, it's the spotting that counts at the start.

As their English teacher, of course I was desperate to get them interested in reading. There is no doubt that confident literacy is crucial to a flourishing adult life. At the worst end, The National Literacy Trust has identified that 60 percent of our prison population have difficulties in basic literacy skills. There is abundant research available on this. A recent Home Office study, 'Evaluation of Basic Skills Training For Prisoners' (Stuart, D.) which accurately benchmarked convicts on entry to Her Majesty's Prisons, found that 55 percent of males were below Literacy Level 1 (which is what you would expect of an 11-year-old). The link between ill-functioning literacy and low self-esteem in adults not only features heavily in studies of inmates, but is staggeringly consistent with petty crime and police attention in teenagers. I introduced the boys to all sorts of stories I thought might interest them. No luck. They were easily bright enough to develop a perspective on themselves through a story (who isn't?), it was just a case of getting them to shut up and listen to the right story. Not an easy task. It took me four and a half months to achieve a real breakthrough, but we got there.

I was trying with little success, to get them to write thoughtful descriptions of people ('He's got a massiv nose like a penis' etc), so I wrote a paragraph on each of them without revealing any physical details. The task was for them to read these descriptions and work out who was which. They devoured this short activity and spent the rest of the lesson in discussion of each other. It was the first time they left the room with their work instead of discarding it on the desk. Two of them came back later and asked for an extra copy. Writing these descriptions gave us our entry point into reading. Who doesn't love hearing interesting things about themselves? They'd felt a bit excited about their education for once. It was tailored just for them. The fact that the boys were captivated by complex language and ideas in these initial descriptions and were willing to discuss themselves and their relationships with one another showed me their strong academic potential and their depth of thought. It sowed a seed.

In his excellent book 'To be a boy, to be a reader', Professor W G Brozo highlights the many risks to boys who fail to engage in reading before they reach adulthood. He insists that the primary goal in using any book is to capture a young man's imagination and keep him reading. The evidence suggests that early and cumulative reading and learning failure are often precursors to unemployment, crime, drug addiction, homelessness and jail.

"Boys who are only 'doing time', who are mentally absent from school and who are mentally detached place themselves and all society at risk…Trying to spark a reluctant boy to read can be a full-time, often frustrating enterprise for parents and other adults. Male youth often find themselves in a handicapping cycle that begins with peer pressure that urges them to avoid reading because it's not 'cool'. This disuse brings on a disdain for reading because it is associated with incompetence and vulnerability. This disdain causes boys to form a mask of indifference to reading, which leads to a further decline in reading ability … The top priority for all teachers and adults is to help boys find entry points into literacy; they should support any way that this can be accomplished." Brozo 2002.

*The above history is extracted from my statement to the disciplinary hearing panel and is no longer confidential; it is available in public records at the City of Leeds Employment Tribunal Service. Still I think that is more than enough of the history part; it is hardly the kind of reading that would encourage any of my boys to go on with active literacy. I wrote this book for and about real people, in their own idiom, to encourage them to read – so it is high time I got on to the story, which in the spirit of History I have set out in the style of its original delivery, with the teacherly drone of lessons between chapters.*

*Well obviously it's all made up, as far
as I know they don't even smoke ...*

*Preface to the original book
August 2008*

# Stop! Don't read this!
## Chapter 1

Greg was feeling shitty that day. Like he was sick of the world not giving him credit, or like things didn't go quite how he planned last night. So he got ready slowly like he wanted to miss the bus.

"Still," he thought, "at least I've got my beloved English teacher period one ... "

Greg has a lot of influence on how things go and a way of walking and talking like he's got a lot in reserve. Like it's worth saving himself for something worthwhile. Like somehow he knows it is going to be okay. There's something very smart about his appearance that makes you think that if he were an actor, he'd play the Cute Guy from the Posh School; I should also mention that Greg looks like he is stronger than he looks.

Billy was thinking in a different way, but thinking the same thing. You know like you do when you wake up; weighing up the things worth getting up for and the things worth shutting out. Billy likes to kid himself that everything's great – and let's face it, it's not a bad way to be when you see what you get out of a day these days. He always has the energy to get things jumping, which is not a great help when you're up against a class like this one. Billy's a bit of a big mouth and I've seen how some kids tense up around him, so I know the lazy way he sometimes flirts with me is just one side of a whole lot of sides. I did once see Billy quiet and still for more than an hour and I learned more about him then than I ever have before. He came to sit in my classroom after he'd been kicked out of someone else's. He looked like he needed a break from everyone and maybe from himself as well. On the day this all started, he blazed in like he usually does with his Ten Man Walk and his Cheshire Cat Grin that sure beats the staff room for a cheerful start to the morning.

Travis is the same but different again. He has eyes the colour of something from long, long ago and he must have Minotaur blood in him or something to be so stacked at sixteen. He comes in like a stranger enters a saloon, like he's expecting loaded guns under the tables. There's a Russian saying…What do you get if you mix three kilos of jam with three kilos of shit? Well the answer is of course six kilos of shit. When Travis is feeling defensive he talks like he had all six kilos for breakfast. He can pack a lot of scorn (and if you don't know what 'scorn' is – just ask him what he thought of his ex-best mate's girlfriend when they were still going out, then bottle his answer, and that … is scorn!) When he comes in chin down, looking at you from under his eyebrows, you can expect a list of swearwords like he's got them belted into an AK47. But not that day. That day he was in one of his sweetie-moods: chatty, funny, encouraging. I have to say though, even when he's in his best mood he is totally unstoppable and he can talk like a burning car that's been shoved off the edge and is crashing through everything on its way down the mountain.

And then there's Christie. It's kind of hard to tell what Christie is thinking. He's got so into the habit of covering his feelings. But what I love about him is the way he's up for returning a smile and how pleased he is when things get funny – and things 'get funny' pretty quickly in this class, but that all depends which side of the laugh you're on. Sometimes he looks like it's kind of a shock for him to find he's in school. Like he has no idea how he got there. I feel the same way occasionally.

I left Martin till last, because even when he comes in first he acts like he's slipping in after everyone else. But once you've noticed Martin, you'd never miss him in a crowd. You have to be sure of yourself to love Martin easily, because he's perfected a way of looking at you like he has not one scrap of warmth for you anywhere inside him. Still, I guess we learn everything from somewhere. I like to think it's someone else's look not his. He uses it to establish no-man's land around him when it seems necessary. But it feels like your birthday when he cracks you a smile.

It was never boring being in a class with those guys, but it was more like an acid trip than a class. For a start you could never even be sure how big it was – which is a fairly typical problem on a trip so I'm told. Sometimes the class was as big as one person (when the Exclusion Room had taken its cut) and sometimes it was like Bring a Friend Day and they were followed in by mates who'd slipped through the system somewhere else. Sometimes there was Jago who is another story altogether but he kind of fits the mould, even though he's younger, so we let him stay. I like the way the boys treat Jago. It shows their softer side. In the early days of our English lessons, anything that showed their softer side was useful, coz they didn't show it to me! More about Jago later.

It wasn't only the class that changed size, the boys changed size as well. They were at that kind of age. Travis was sometimes a tall kid and sometimes when he was angry his head touched the ceiling like Alice in Wonderland. Billy was supposed to be officially short but I often felt like he was way taller than me, and they all melted into the furniture if the office monitor pitched up with the Detention List. Sometimes five minutes could seem like an hour, or forty minutes could go in one second. Sometimes they brought the weather in with them and sometimes it seemed as if their arms were on fire (well, just that one time with the Lynx. Jee-sus). Surreal moments. As I say, the whole thing was more like a trip than a class.

It was even weird how the boys turned up. Not like it usually is in our school, with a line-up by a door after a bell. It sometimes felt like I never actually saw the boys arrive: I'd be walking with one and then suddenly there'd be three of them and everything kind of became a group. Like the unspoken communication was strong in that gang. Like everyone knew the plan without discussing it. In school anyway.

Maybe we should have realized, that every school day can't be 'Just Another Normal School Day' every day. Sometimes there has to be a one-off. This one was going to be different and they were going to be in the thick of it. I remembered afterwards walking happily along the library corridor in formation with the boys, before all the madness started, smiling a smile to myself and thinking,

'I wonder if they know they are my favourites. And I wonder if they know why?'

*  *  *

It's no accident, the closeness between the words 'history' and 'story'. Some languages have the same word for both. Any bit of history could begin with 'Once upon a time'. I mean, look at the times we are living in now, not much of a fairytale I know, but I was an English teacher once upon a time and if you put me in a classroom for a couple of minutes, I could probably spot you at least an Ugly Duckling, a Cinderella and one of those Princes who got turned into a frog.

I should confess that I don't have a degree in English. I got a couple of A's for my GCSEs and that's about it on the official English front. I grew up in the countryside, my dad shot the TV after catching me and my brother watching 'mindless rubbish' when we should have been doing our homework, and we had to resort to all the mouldy old books lying around for entertainment. I read a lot. Later I travelled a lot, talking to anyone I could find along the way. I liked that the world is made up of stories, and that people tell them everywhere, every day to share their human experiences with one another. People learn smoothly from stories. I was never religious, but I respect old Jesus as an English teacher. As far as I can tell, he sat around a lot weaving yarns and asking people comprehension questions till they understood the lesson (although not in English of course).

I wandered into teaching via my circuitous international route. All that talking to people from other cultures improved my foreign languages, so when I gave up Wandering as a general occupation and settled down near my parents to raise a family, teaching French and German at a local school seemed like a respectable use of my skills. It didn't take long for me to realise that teaching foreign languages to the majority of English kids takes a particular brand of dogged determination and a rhino-hided devotion to a predominantly lost cause which I don't appear to have. It's lovely teaching the younger ones, who still find it fun to

18

*play lotto or form simple sentences describing the position of a cat in relation to various pieces of bedroom furniture, but as the years go by, and in the absence of any good French hip hop on the iPods of our youth, the gap between what they can say and what they want to say widens beyond frustration. They just don't see the point. Trying to justify my subject got in the way of my growing love for teaching, so I switched from foreign languages to teaching English. It sounds like a cop-out I know, but I'm a great believer in adapting to the terrain and although I live in hope that one day more English speakers will find the value of communicating in other tongues, it's not about to happen in the current system I'm afraid. It doesn't end there though. Given the prevalent perception of teenagers as a bit of an alien species both in and out of schools, it's like they are another culture in themselves that, as grown ups, we have to learn a language to comprehend. In their turn of course, young people have to learn a new language and culture in order to grow into adults.*

*I'd spent a whole decade learning my craft to a standard that was worth something. It wasn't easy. Like any activity you undertake, there are points along the way where you could just settle for being proficient in your league, or you could risk failure in an effort to level up. Teaching is no exception. It is a steady job in a solid structure and after a couple of bewildering years you have enough skills to satisfy the standards of Continuing Professional Assessment. You have a punishment system at your disposal, so you gain reasonable control and you have a lot of knowledge to fill out the hours of a timetable. Whether you are a good teacher or a poor one you have to do a lot of work, and although many have tried, there seems to be no way to avoid this. The profession acknowledges within itself that it is a bottomless pit. However much you put in, there is more to do – so if you are perfect at the paperwork for example, you don't have a lot of time for other aspects of the job. As you become more experienced, you learn to manage the workload by having surges of enthusiasm for different tasks depending on the expediency. It's a precarious way to live really. Very little marking goes on while you are running a school show, or taking thirty twelve-year-olds to France. The impossibility of doing the whole job all the time results in a constant hunted feeling which you whittle down to a bearable size by neglecting the things which seem least important. Helping students find their way is hard to quantify, and paperwork is easily monitored. As you can imagine, it is safer to cover the paperwork and leave the less target-specific work undone, unless you have the kind of spirit that sleeps fitfully on such a choice that is.*

*I can't say enough about how much I admire teenagers. I appreciate it's not a popular opinion these days, and if you are not sick of my enthusiasm for them by the end of this paragraph, you may well be by the end of the book. In my time as a teacher, I discovered teenagers to be a band of spiritual idealists the like of which it's practically impossible to find in the adult world in any significant concentration of numbers. I know teenagers are ultra stress-head drama-mongers who contradict everything including themselves. That they often have utterly baffling notions as to the quantity of make-up one face can support whilst allowing the rest of the body only the most minimal protection from the rigours of climate. They speak harshly and use F-words in place of more traditional punctuation, and can down absolutely anything that has been deemed too sickly for human consumption and left to fester at the back of a drinks cabinet. Sometimes they lie and steal and poke wounded creatures with sticks for entertainment. They fight, and scare old ladies just by their very existence in multiples on streets, and they have a terrifying hedonistic curiosity for dangerous, if amusing, illegal substances. Teenagers are also the undisputed champions of the door-slam and the stomp-off, but it's tough work being a spiritual idealist. No wonder most of us give it up. We can still remember at times, whether we admit it or not, how it feels to be a teenager in the thrall of evolutionary thrust: all those burning passions and smarting dreams that made us so hard for our parents to live with. What I find so special about teenagers, is that they believe in change and can flourish under the smallest kindness. They have hope, however well hidden, and they treasure simple, beautiful things. They are not so far past fairytales that they have ruled out magical intervention. Every single one of them knows a piece of music which can lift them out of their ordinary existence for a few short minutes and turn crap into gold. Like water on a flat school roof, they can find their way through anything, and the amount of strain from within and without that they can put up with whilst still returning a genuine smile with interest is astounding. (If you doubt me on that last one – doubt your smile!) Discovering teenagers helped me to discover myself. It took a while for me to find the way, but they salvaged my ideals before it was too late and I will personally be grateful to them as a species for all eternity.*

*Anyone who has never made a mistake,*
*has never tried anything new.*

*Albert Einstein*

*My class was a dumping ground for the most difficult Year 11 boys; they were all regarded as unteachable for one reason or another, in fact really at the beginning of the year they came across as little more than charismatic shits. So much for first impressions. I'd never met anyone as bitter about education as they were. They were sick of teachers squaring up to them with their flat eyes and their power shields. By the end of the first week back in September, the boys had enough detentions lined up between them to start their own school. Where do you go from there? I had to get through to them somehow. That's how this story really started. I could find you all sorts of deeper beginnings, but I think the fact that Greg was actually feeling very shitty that day is somehow the key to it all. That, and the fact that I wanted a way to tell him that I knew how he was feeling, and that I had a fair idea why. They were nobody's favourites in school so I suppose I made them mine. Officially we like the people who behave well in life, but if you look at the History of the World, it's the troublemakers we honour in the end. Someone once said, disobedience is a great thing, because disobedience and rebellion change the world. I like that. And the world is in need of a change for sure. When you are a kid, you should have a right to help from adults, however much help you need. I firmly believe it takes a lot for a kid to become that difficult, and what it takes doesn't come from within.*

*Back in the day when they were twelve-year-olds I had these boys for French of all things. They were hard work, but they had such bright, cheeky little faces and they were so full of life, I couldn't ever be annoyed with them for long. One time when I'd completely had it with their mayhem, I made them all stare silently at the wall for the rest of the lesson. I felt like such a dick and I thought they'd never forgive me. It's pathetic when you've got all that power and you run out of ideas. Sometimes you get angrier with the kids when deep down you wish you had come* up with a better lesson for them. I guess you can't always sparkle can you? Anyway, every time I saw one of them in the corridor after that, they'd shout things like,

"Are we gonna do Staring At The Wall again next lesson Miss?!" like they were really looking forward to it. Funny guys. That's when I started reading them a story on Friday if they did French the rest of the week. It kind of worked. They still didn't learn much French, but we suddenly had a nice time in lessons instead of a headfuck. We had found something in common. I still get a lump in my throat when I remember how much Christie loved stories.

It was in their final year of school that the boys challenged me to write a story about them. Any bunch of teenagers is a tough audience for your own personal creativity and the Commy Boys were about as tough an audience as you could get. Seriously, you have no idea how good these guys were at cutting you down to size. It's easy to get defensive around disaffected kids. They make you feel so rejected. I didn't want to have to stand up in class and read out my work to a gang of serious hard-core piss-takers.

It got to me though, the state of those guys in the classroom. Especially after knowing them when they were younger. Their outsides had hardened so much. I didn't want to disappoint them. I can't stand to see kids lose hope, and it's a huge thing for proud people who feel like they get nothing from the system to actually ask for anything, never mind something as far from 'street' as a story. Sadly in the modern world it is only children who have stories read to them and the boys had to admit they were children to ask for a story. This required a lot of faith from them and an acceptance of me as their teacher rather than as just some smiley woman with a tolerance for unfair treatment. I was torn.

*I remember once talking to a class about earliest memories. The subject came up in some book we were reading. I've noticed that small things kids remember from childhood are sometimes like bookmarks for bigger things which were too unpleasant to keep in their heads. For example, my earliest memory is of lying in an unfamiliar bed with my mum and hearing an owl hoot outside the window. I only know now that I had just had a hefty operation. Some kids remember things like sitting on a large sofa stroking a sleeping dog rather than that it was their grandma's, and that she had just died. It's a blessing to be protected by your memory in your most formative time, to be allowed to learn what really happened years later over a cup of tea and a photo album or something. It's not like that for everyone though. One kid told us his earliest memory was of his dad leaving. He'd been taken to the toyshop and told he could choose whatever he wanted. He'd chosen a flash toy car, but his dad said it was too expensive and got something else instead, before leaving him with one of those overwet kisses on the cheek that you want to wipe off. He couldn't remember what the toy was, and he never saw his father again. The kids with safer memories tried not to stare, like we try not to stare at car crashes on the opposite carriageway. That boy was an ebullient, dangerous, golden troublemaker who got in the way of progress in just about every lesson he ever bothered to attend, but on days like that when he put his faith in us and joined in, he taught us things about the world that we would never forget.*

*Maybe I should have been a bit more careful about offering my class the choice of the whole toyshop, but I really wanted to give them something to help them forgive their education. I didn't want to let them down, but I was at a loss for what kind of story I could possibly write to interest them. I stressed over it all week, till I took my dog Zoomo for a walk across some moonlit fields and began to feel all inspired. You don't have to be soft in the head to think that there is something special about moonlight.*

*It brings out faster and exciting thoughts. Like they are there all around you in darkness anyway, but the moonlight shows them up.*

*You can get some pretty unclipped ideas in moonlight.*

*I was thinking about this bit in Harry Potter (yes I like Harry Potter, so what? I really like it!) this bit where this kid finds out his best mate is a werewolf. I suppose it could happen to anyone. Werewolves have to deal with a lot of prejudice. People hate them, even though they don't choose to become werewolves. Usually it's just a case of being in the wrong place at the wrong time. Anyway I bet no-one would've blamed this kid if he had just dissed the wolfboy at that point, but he didn't. Instead, he learned to turn himself into a dog so that he could run alongside his werewolf friend and keep him out of trouble. Stop him chewing up chicks and all that, but without getting chewed up himself.*

*See, that is the kind of loyalty that really counts for something. I mean, hardly anyone can turn themselves into a dog, let's face it. It must have taken a lot of hard work. I shouldn't really compare the boys to werewolves, even though I'm sure they would admit it got A BIT WILD at times, but I really wanted to write a story that would turn me into a dog. So I could run alongside them, and maybe even keep them out of trouble. I liked the idea of a story where we didn't have to be on separate sides. If we were at war in the classroom maybe a story in which we were the characters could provide us with a meeting point on a neutral plane. It would give me a way to step into their world and show them I knew who they were. You have to know who kids really are and love them anyway to have any impact. I got to thinking that in the name of stories you can say what you wouldn't normally say, and show what you wouldn't normally show. I admit I also kind of liked the idea that an OFSTED inspector could come and look through the toughened glass door panel of my classroom and see five quiet boys listening and a teacher droning on at the front. Just as it should be. We would all be looking nice and chilled, while the boys were actually getting up to some crazy stuff as usual, but safe in the story rather than in real life. I mean isn't that what education is supposed to be, an escape? These boys were fairly keen on escaping the classroom anyway, so escaping it into an education could marry my agenda with theirs ... Brilliant!*

*Well that was the general idea, but you know how it is with inspirational walks: you get home, you shut the door. You're home. So when Thursday came around I bottled it completely and wrote them a silly story about Billy the Goat and his forest friends. It was a cowardly effort to back out of the bargain. I felt like I'd nicely side-stepped a vulnerable position by using a bit of humour to hide the fact that I was wimping out on the challenge.*

*I knew I'd made a major mistake as soon as I got to the classroom. They were all there before me. A first. They were all sitting down. Inconceivable. They demanded their story and shushed each other to hear what I'd come up with. You should have seen the contempt on their faces when I read out 'The Woodland Massacre.' Travis the Squirrel for god's sake! Talk about woodland animals, I felt like such a rat. They'd asked for something, shown an interest and I had let them down. They were so scathing about the story. I don't blame them. They argued bitterly about my choice of animals, attaching all sorts of negative significance to the various species in question. Greg still hasn't forgiven me for making him a fox.*

*That's the way it goes I suppose. Sometimes you get scared to try in case you fail and everyone knows you tried. I hate it when that happens to me. 'The Woodland Massacre' was an epic fail, so I had to give it another shot. I was in my usual place between them and the whiteboard, listening to their chat: Greg on feeling shitty, Christie on the subject of his day ... and I just wrote on from there. It seemed like the only place with any meeting point of relevance for us. Truth is it's not really effective to play it safe around people who are well past safe.*

Our lesson that day went pretty much how Thursday mornings seemed to go. Travis dissolved into my form room sometime in registration and the rest materialized out of somewhere or other on the way to 'the Ghetto', the scruffiest classroom in school, but it's good enough for us and can take the kind of hard knocks it gets if the boys are feeling 'antsy'.

'The Ghetto' (seriously you should see the state of my classroom) certainly suited the derelict mood Greg couldn't seem to shake off: flat out across the desk, using his arms as a pillow, turning to face the rest occasionally to offer some comment, then turning away again towards the wall. He's a funny one Greg. He doesn't trust you to like him and he's always on the look out for evidence that you don't. He shows you've offended him very quietly and he measures you by how long it takes you to notice. You can't talk down to Greg if you want to get anywhere. And it's hard to get anywhere with him if he doesn't want you to get anywhere.

We were supposed to be reading this book called 'The Loneliness of the Long Distance Runner'. It's a great book. Long title I know, but the kid in the story had a long way to run. Bit depressing as well, but the boys were mostly looking so miserable I thought it might have been 'on their vibe' or something. You wouldn't believe how many books I'd tried with these guys. Tough crowd! Anyway, they weren't having it. We got through about a page and a half and then 'zWRyoOOP!!' (This is the point where there should be a way to spell that 'zWRyooP!' sound you get when you whack the arm of a record deck right across a tune and it scratches into silence in the middle of the record. Usually means the end of the party. It's that same sound I get in my head when I'm interrupted while I'm reading aloud. ZWRyooP!!) And I thought it was going so well, getting through a whole page and a half...

"I can't be doing with this at all!" Greg breaks in, like it has been a major battle to put up with five minutes of book (gotta say though I appreciate the effort!) "It just does my head in all that crap!! Who cares what some guy is thinking while he's running across a field for fuck's sake!!"

So we headed to the vendor for hot chocolate. My treat. It's worth every penny, not only for the corridor roaming but when they sit there drinking it, they suddenly all look like sons. (Not MY sons, but somebody's sons. And when you see someone as a son, they really start to matter). It helps me get over my frustration and there's no point fighting them, they're way better at fighting than me.

Billy was talking about how he would feel if he had a daughter and she was a slag. He can put on such a hard front. Like when some random kid sticks its head round the door of the classroom to sound off about some triumph or some trauma it reckons it's just had, Billy can slay them in a sentence. Then the poor random kid will kind of wilt and skulk away. It's a Billy Special. When he's on a level with you though, you can really get some deep shit out of Billy. Seems like he's thinking a lot about the world these days. He can rap on for hours on the subject of slags, but he wouldn't like to see his own daughter turn out that way. He started in, like he does, on what girls are fit for. I tried to get the subject on to a classier level, by asking if he's ever had any finer feelings for a girl. Billy is a great talker, he holds his crowd in spite of the swearing, and how far past appropriate he gets in the first line…

*Billy on the subject of Finer Feelings:*

*"Fuck finer feelings! What finer feeling is there than a good shag ey Miss?!" HAAH!*

Hmmm! Then he gets on to telling us about this girl he liked at primary school in the pre-erection days when a long-term relationship lasted through from playtime to dinner. When holding hands with some scabby-kneed 'girl next door' was like ultimate pride and contentment. Awwww. Surprised us all. There was a rare moment of quiet when he finished his speech, just an occasional slurp of hot chocolate here and there. We were all wondering about where that feeling goes maybe. Or whether it ever comes back. I was watching Billy, rocked right back on his chair, balanced at an impossible angle, blue eyes flashing round, watching to challenge any challenge from the group. For once there was none. So who knows, when he's had his young man's fun he might start seeing more of the long lost primary school angels of this world and start treating them more like someone's daughter. Well yeah, maybe after quite a few years of young man's fun let's face it.

Martin sloped in well after the others. Like he'd been in two minds whether to give it a miss. But like I said before, once you've noticed Martin you wouldn't forget him so we've brought him chocolate just in case. Almost anything for a smile from Martin. He's so guarded with his approval. When he does come out with some thought or feeling it's like he's speaking for the first time, and you get a little look at just how much there is about Martin. I can see why some people find him unnerving though. Maybe they haven't seen the smile! Can't say I've seen much of it myself but I have a good memory for nice things, which has to count for something in a class full of bullies.

We still hadn't done any work though. I don't know how the hell I'm supposed to get them back on reading after Greg has damned the book for all eternity after a page and a half.

I looked around. Martin had his headphones on (at a reasonable volume to be fair). He could still hear what was going on because Billy was filling him in on something. Travis had a secret. You could just tell. It was more than just looking a bit high. He looked like nothing that was said to him could affect him much. Like whatever it was he was turning over in his head was cushioning him from the outside world. Travis can get pretty heated, so it's obvious something is going on with him and there seems to be a link with Billy's rant about girls. It's a bit early in the morning for Christie to be awake, in fact he's doing a fair good impression of the dormouse in the teapot at the Mad Hatter's tea party, that just wakes up every now and again and looks cute and sleepy but unwilling to face the cold light of day for long. Smiley though.

See I can't help sympathizing with them and how pissed off they are with school. They do special courses at the local college half the week and are expected to be kids again on Thursday and Friday. Still, you have to try.

"Why won't you let me read to you boys? The whole world is made up of stories."

They must have caught the note of desperation in my voice coz they all looked at me a bit concerned for once.

"I told you, it just does my head in all that crap," says Greg like he's talking me down from a high window ledge. I still felt like jumping.

"Well what am I supposed to do with you?" I'm looking for an answer here.

"Tell you what, we'd listen if you wrote a story about us. About how we feel every day and our life at school". Christie is quite enthusiastic all of a sudden. "I reckon all English teachers should be able to write stories. It shows they're good at English."

"Yeah, and then make something exciting happen!" It's a rare one for Billy to follow Christie's lead on an idea, I have to admit. A rare one.

Travis is into it as well, which is dangerous for me coz he just wears you down when he wants his way,

"I know you read us stories in year eight, but it's hardly the same now is it. You're gonna have to up the stakes."

"Yeah then we'd listen; but you'd better make it good!" Greg adds.

Martin just sat quietly; second row, by the wall.

I let them go a bit early in the end. Well, I say I let them go; they did one of those mass departures without even discussing it. Like someone just pulled an imaginary plug and they start heading for the plughole.

* * *

*There's a movie called* Legally Blonde *about an archetypal Malibu Barbie girl who majors in fashion at college in California until her boyfriend dumps her to go to Harvard Law School and she decides she is going to go there too to get him back. On the face of it, it is a classic girly college movie, a feel-gooder with a lot of pink in it; in spite of this I'd put it in my top ten favourite movies of all time. Elle Woods, the protagonist, is ridiculed for her fluffy pens, her immaculately accessorised chihuahua and her obsessive value for appearance. She is a ditsy expert on fashion and struggles to be taken seriously by the real law students who disparage her way of assessing people on their philosophy of hair, the quality of their high-kicks or their attitudes towards eyebrow maintenance. Eventually of course Elle solves a high profile murder case when she realises the key witness could not have been in the shower when her father was shot, because she had just come home from having a perm. Elle moves from struggling to remember the right legal terms, to being a strong and capable adversary when she finds herself on ground she is sure of. She completely upskittles the witness into confessing to the murder, believing beyond any shadow of a doubt that no self-respecting daughter would shower at such a time, because of the risk of de-activating the ammonium thioglycolate.*

*I loved this movie for its emphasis on playing to your strengths. I used it as an assembly and as a lesson plan to state my message to kids- find what you are good at, and go for it. Honour what you excel at and allow it to bring you confidence in all aspects of your life. It was a long time before I realised that I could look at this from the other side. It's all too easy as a viewer to identify with the heroine and feel proud of yourself for appreciating her, but a teacher in real life runs the risk of being more like the law students and tutors in the movie who looked down on Little Miss Manicure. We are good at telling young people what they should do to achieve more, while we forget that there are things*

35

*beyond horizons. We see kids who are rude, unruly, tempera-
mental and we think they are hopeless cases who are incapable
of behaving properly. How can we reinvent a person's behaviour
in three lessons a week? They are generally to be excluded or
punished down to acceptably containable levels. We can't expect
to do much more.*

*We had a staff training day one time with some guy who taught
us positive visualisation. He said that if you take two minutes
before a difficult class and close your eyes and imagine them how
you would like them to be, your brain has a level to aim for and
you set a standard for them which is closer to the ideal image.
By keeping the goal in mind, you reach it. Of course we all joked
afterwards about nipping into the corridor at change of lessons
to assume the lotus position amidst the trampling feet, to light
a bit of incense and dream of our kids poncing in wearing little
straw boater hats and blazers, and depositing kilos of apples
and copperplate homework on our desks. The visualisation idea
isn't a silly one though, the problem is that it works the other
way without even trying. I had bought into the reputation of the
Commy Boys as legends; somehow we viewed them as different
to other kids. Something to defend ourselves from. Something to
be survived.*

*In the first few harrowing weeks of my lessons with the Commy
Boys, I was forced to think a lot about how I felt in my failure
to engage them. I was a popular, experienced, kindly teacher,
accustomed to being warmed to; I came to the conclusion that
the way they ignored me hurt. I felt like I didn't deserve it, and it
made me want a way to hurt them back so they would know how
it felt. As if they didn't know how it felt! Exclusion, punishment
and the good old Guilt Trip didn't work, because they were so
used to being excluded and punished that they had found a way
to be impregnable – they just excluded and punished me first.
They ganged up on me to make me look stupid and they had*

36

*insider jokes and were nice to each other while I stood on my own at the front. I began to realise that by routinely demonising young people who could really use the most help, we are teaching them how to hurt us. They learn to find our weak spots and our vulnerabilities by blocking up their own. As I felt more and more defensive, I worried over the issue of weak spots. It didn't feel right to be cementing mine over. It didn't feel right, because teaching is a mirror.*

*We need weaknesses. They are the parts of us where change can happen. You can't be moved without having weak spots. You dare not think and dream sweet things. Without them people grow in the opposite direction to what is great about mankind. Weak spots are actually the strength of our species. I don't even know why we call them weaknesses – rather a negative word for powerful things like Faith and Trust if you ask me, and anyway you have to risk having points where people can break in, to have points where you can break out. Entry points and exit points are the same. If you can't expose them at sometime or another you are trapped, and all you can do is grow inwards. Weak spots are windows of opportunity. They are the gateways for change and children should be able to trust their adults to guard them whilst they traffic with new experiences.*

*I cared about the Commy Boys before I started writing the story. I was scared of them like everyone else, and I didn't know how to handle them, but I was impressed by the fact that they refused to have their spirit crushed by us telling them how appalling they were all the time. When I finished reading them the first chapter, I got all the proof I needed of who they really were. If there had been anything unsalvageable or mean about any one of those boys they could have pounced right then while I was totally disarmed. If they were interested in winning they could have won. I'd never have been able to face them again if they had ridiculed my work.*

*I couldn't even look at them in the silence that followed, but I'd already started to understand that they disparaged our bad opinion of them for its limited view, and that they rejected us because we failed them. What the hell are we doing to our kids! I'm not saying it was all sunshine, lollipops and rainbows from that point, but I knew, like you do, that I'd started to love them. I was still nervous before every class for a long time after that. It was a habit I suppose – like a horse being led under a tree that once had a lion in it. Or something that smelled like a lion. Or something the other horses warned was a lion. A bunch of lion-coloured foals bound together and hoisted up the lion tree.*

# Stop! Don't read this!
## Chapter 2

I wonder how things would have turned out differently if the boys hadn't gone noisily out of my door nine minutes before the bell, and they hadn't gone through the yard (which was a rare one for them as they generally go the other way round the building to avoid confrontations near the staffroom), and if Greg hadn't booted the bin over as his mood failed to improve despite a quiet start to the day, and if the caretaker hadn't come round the corner just at that moment in the kind of temper when a caretaker least wants to see another of his bins booted over....

He came out fierce anyway, like an ogre from its cave and had somehow managed to get the boys into his office and sitting down for a good amount of hassle, before anyone realized what was happening. He must've really meant it because it's not easy to get the construction group boys to do something they would rather not do, whoever you are. They gave up investing in people's good books a while ago.

So, the caretaker started to follow up his advantage and have a good old shout to relieve the stresses of the week. This wasn't going to get him very far as the boys have a low tolerance level for being shouted at. They've seen it all before. But just when he was really starting to get into his stride, the phone rang. He stopped mid-sentence and looked at the receiver like it was loaded, before answering it in a phoney-cheerful way.

The boys were left to stare past him at the ranks of security screens with school on every channel: corners of corridors, and perimeter doors, and acres of dining hall, and stripy bits of staircases. The caretaker sounds like someone is giving it to him like he was giving it to the boys himself a moment ago. He's trying to chip in and calm down whoever he's talking to. It starts to sound urgent.

"Fuck this," mutters Greg under his breath, "I'm gonna do one. I'm not in the mood for this at all." Travis is quick to agree to the idea and the others stir a bit.

"Ey look at that!" says Martin quietly. He hasn't taken his eyes off the screens since they came in. They followed where he was looking, to a screen on the bottom row showing a staircase.

"Gyms," confirms Travis as if the question had been asked. When they look closely, they can see a couple of girls under the staircase going through a bag. They are tearing up the books in it and putting them back.

"Wonder whose bag it is?" says Christie, not expecting an answer particularly, but it reminds you that he's no stranger to people doing shit things. Billy cracks out a sudden loud laugh as he spots someone he knows getting told off on another screen. The caretaker glowers at him as he attempts to get whoever it is off the phone. Eventually he hangs up and swings round to tell the boys they have to wait till he gets back or they will be in big trouble. It must have been a seriously gippy phone call because he is out of the door without even stopping to think whether or not it was really a good idea to leave the boys in his office, especially after shouting at them. It doesn't take long to go through a desk, but the boys were all focused on the screens now. They were watching a kid trying to get in through the perimeter doors with a dodgy security fob, and doing a bit of commentating.

The girls in the first screen had left the bag now and it lay as if unharmed at the bottom of the steps. Girls have plenty ways to make girls suffer.

'The bag probably belonged to their best friend,' thought Greg, but he didn't say it out loud.

It doesn't take long before they've sussed out which bits are worth watching, where the action is and where there are cameras they never knew about. They are the kind of boys who are used to checking out such things quickly. They are sharp like that.

Then Travis sights the caretaker scurrying past the main boys' toilets looking more and more like his day was no fun, and they started seeing who could predict which screen he'd turn up on next. Martin called it three times in a row, but Christie got the best one when he somehow predicted a u-turn, and the caretaker confirmed it by turning up again in a screen he'd just left.

Finally he stopped and they saw him hurrying to unlock the door of room M6 before disappearing inside. They waited but he didn't come out. The game seemed to be over, but they all continued to stare at the screen. Billy got a lighter out of his pocket and started flicking it on over and over. Travis shifted around a bit. Still no caretaker.

"Let's just get out of here while he's at the other end of school," Greg suggested, and the pack stirred to its feet. Being stuck in some mouldy office waiting for another power trip wasn't exactly anyone's idea of a good time.

"He's left his keys in the door," said Martin as they took one last look at the screen.

They streamed out and headed off towards the main office but on sighting Mrs. Foulds, they doubled back towards the Maths department. Meeting the caretaker again would be preferable to an encounter with her after the other day. I don't know what they'd done exactly but I doubt she had forgotten.

Greg was taking his mood out on Christie for some reason and so was Travis for some other reason and one way or another they ended up on the approach to M6. It's one of those things about being a kid, you always seem to end up heading straight towards what you think you'd rather avoid. The caretaker was still inside and they sped up to get by unnoticed. As they passed, one by one, the large bunch of keys gleamed at them like a world of openable doors, and memories of the recent chewing out that the caretaker had given them made the boys keen for a bit of vengeance. Christie was last. They got through the doors at the end of the corridor and all turned again to look at the keys. There was a silence. Then Travis said,

"We should just nick 'em. I bet he won't even remember where he left them. He was in a right state".

There was another silence and Christie had the unpleasant feeling that everyone was looking at him. He tried to ignore it but it wouldn't go away. What a day.

"Why do I have to do it?" he asked no-one in particular. But he already knew the job had fallen to him. Sometimes when you get a job to do, even if it isn't really a job you wanted, you have an inspiration about doing it well. Christie must have had one of those inspired moments as he walked back up the corridor to M6, with the rest of the boys staying round him, keeping up the pressure.

The others took off down the corridor as soon as Christie's hand closed round the keys. He'd committed himself by then. It took him a bit of time to get the keys out of the lock and the others were back through the double doors before he caught them up. Everyone likes a good run down the corridor so they kept going.

"He won't be chasing us anyway," said Christie as they came bursting out into the senior yard.

"Why not?" Greg asked.

"I locked him in!"

Nice one Christie. I like it when he gets approval, coz Christie has a lot of spirit really. They left the yard noisily and headed towards the park. Greg was now fully recovered from his mood of earlier and was telling his entertaining stories of 'the other night' like he does. Travis was glad to be out in the open, Martin was happy on the move.

It was Billy who remembered the camera that would implicate them completely for stealing the keys. Damn. How many last, final, very last, totally final warnings could they have? This could mean the end of school before the year had properly begun. They walked on in silence for a while contemplating the problem and coming out with occasional well-chosen swearwords.

"You know what, it isn't really a problem anymore though now we've got these," said Billy and he jangled the caretaker's keys. They made a good jangle. So they should with the master keys, and the fobs, and all the perimeter keys, and the alarm keys packed onto the ring.

"I think we might be coming back to school tonight to do a bit of TV editing lads…"

Which is how they ended up in school late that night. And how they ended up getting involved in something much heavier than they'd bargained for. They couldn't have predicted what happened next…

*I was right there with Christie on the inspiration for doing a job well, whether you wanted the job or not. We were getting something out of our story. It had to cross a few boundaries or they would have had no excuse to enjoy it. We were getting to know each other on a genuine footing.*

*I used to go with my granny to feed the ducks. I loved it, but there always seemed to be one duck, some daft mallard, who kept missing the bread no matter how well-aimed; like it swam the wrong way, or got in wrangles with the other ducks at the crucial moment. I took the job pretty seriously. I was obsessed with the idea that feeding the ducks had to mean every last one, and my granny had to wait patiently with armfuls of loaves, till the whole raft of them would be just about ready to sink from overfeeding and l finally managed to get some into the bill of the one bloody duck that evolution had apparently given up on.*

*I'm the same about children.. I don't mean I lob bread at them, just that I refuse to see any kid as a lost cause. It goes against everything that a child is. Maybe the duck-thing is a poor example. We have a way more complex social structure than theirs, but the boundaries we seem to have established to protect children can really get in the way of the Bread For Every Last Duck campaign sometimes. They need shifting a bit for the sake of those kids who are squashed right up to the edges. There's still plenty of space in the middle for the majority to munch happily on a regular education. Although I have to say, the boundaries around education these days are getting narrower and narrower in a world that is broadening by the second. It's leaving more than just a few on the ropes.*

*As a teacher you are expected to develop a Classroom Persona. This is supposed to take the form of a sort of sanitised imaginary self to protect the teacher and the students from The Real You. I've always had a bit of a problem with it. A classroom persona is like an imaginary friend which distances its creator from reality. You can blame your imaginary friend for all sorts of failings, or retreat behind him when life is hard to accept. It is beyond our mortal abilities to create a real living being (and for all you pedants out there I'm not talking about babies – any fool can create one of those) what I mean is, that an imaginary friend can't really be expected to match up to all the complex demands of genuine interaction with its real life counterparts. Like a lot of educational ideas, the classroom persona plays towards the home stand. By this I mean it works in a broad sense, but as soon as it meets anything requiring a little more creativity of approach, you may as well sit your local village competition-winning guy fawkes at the front of the classroom, or get Frankenstein's monster in on supply. (or should I say 'Frank Einstein's monster' as a kid once suggested when I held up a photo of the world-renowned theoretical physicist and asked the class if they knew what he was famous for. Awww)*

*The classroom persona might have had its place in the olden days, in the times when old ladies put on their sunday best before firing up the wireless, when people weren't really supposed to be real, and suffering in silence was just what kids did. Before the information superhighway came into the hands of children, they had very little proof of what adult authority figures really were. It is not like that now. Like it or not children know a lot more about what adults are. They know that they swear among their own kind and do all sorts of things not condonable in a classroom. What children are supposed to learn from school is a professional way to behave in a professional setting. There's no real appreciation of the effort that takes for all of us if we have to pretend we don't know any swear words. And still you get teachers, putting all they've got into their performance, and yelling things like, "How dare you say that! I've never heard such language in all my life!" when even the smallest, sweetest child knows that that, is in fact, a load of bobbins.*

*Because you are limited to a role, it's hard to keep in mind that the uniformed children are also real everyday people with real everyday problems. It's not because teachers are mean that they treat children at school so differently from children at home, it's because the system demands that they put a distance between themselves, the students, and reality. It's impossible to keep it up all the time, and when the real person breaks out, it impresses the kids as much as it makes the teacher uncomfortable. The kids want more of it, which makes the teachers all snappy and defensive and before you know it, the punishments are flying around to mend the fence. It's small wonder that in such a difficult emotional job, nothing seems to make sense any more.*

*I'm thinking now about the old worn classic, The Dog That Ate The Homework. No-one's buying it are they, but if you've ever had the very wearing pleasure of bringing up a dog, you'll know that a well done piece of homework is in fact just the sort of thing any self-respecting puppy would go for given the chance. Schools generally read Of Mice and Men for GCSE English. It's an utterly arresting work which touches the hearts of all who get to the end. It's the kind of story that those kids who've read ahead ask you not to finish in class to avoid mass public weeping for the huge dangerous idiot who kills the pretty girl. John Steinbeck, who wrote it, won the Nobel Prize, and there's not an English teacher alive who would dispute he deserved it. When he'd finished writing it he went out for a well-earned whisky or something and came back to find the manuscript mauled beyond recognition by his dog. He probably missed a few deadlines having to re-write the whole book, and who knows whether the first draft ever included that devastating scene where the dog gets shot, but my point is, that while we sympathize with poor old Steinbeck for having to start all over again, you try telling your English teacher your dog ate your Of Mice and Men essay and see where it gets you. Any kid who knows anything about school would think it smarter to make up some lie rather than risk the simple truth on his one shot at avoiding detention.*

*John Steinbeck's 'thing', was understanding. He believed if people took the trouble to truly understand each other, they would be kind to each other. "Knowing a man well never leads to hate and nearly always leads to love." It's a pure and humanitarian ideal, which we have to teach as if it were in a test-tube, unsafe to be let loose in the classroom. Steinbeck may well have been a little sod at school, and maybe it wasn't even true about the dog and the manuscript; he might have been pulling that as a scam for years, but I doubt knowing that would make him any less worthy of respect, it might even make him more.*

*There are constant complaints in the media, in schools and in our communities about the endless problem of disaffected teenage boys, and yet there is still no national strategy for helping them. They are despised, blamed, feared even, and they are still our children. I wonder if people resent them so much because they are such a map of our ailing society. I'm tired of people saying they are their own worst enemy. They are children, and when children are really in a mess, they need to know you are real and that you understand. There is little to be gained from asking for help from a guy fawkes who has been enthusiastically stuffed with policies, government directives and computer-generated reports. It's sad when children know you are officially there to help, and they know you officially can't.*

*I seem to have sacked off my classroom persona. I'm tired of pretending that kids go home at teatime to polish their satchels and lay out their ribbons for tomorrow's tidy plaits, and I don't want to punish people just because my imaginary friend says so. I wanted to be real enough to help kids understand that we are all struggling to survive in a system, and that the good news is, a system can be survived.*

# Stop! Don't read this!
## Chapter 3

So the plan was to meet up behind the technology block at half nine when it would be sure to be dark. As it turned out, it was well dark before nine, and they didn't all get there till after ten. But that's plans for you. Standing together in the road at night, they didn't look as much like a gang. Like you can tell in a bar whether a group of people are out together because they are mates or they're out together coz they work together. Like something outside of them formed the gang, not something inside of them if you know what I mean.

Getting into the building was so easy it was almost a shame. A waste of their collective talent. Not like their raid on the ice-cream van wasn't a waste of collective talent. That kind of pack and grab raid the other week that put me in mind of those dogs called Afghan Hounds, which were bred to race into enemy bandit camps in packs, grabbing ammunition and weapons and even the dinner off the fire before making off into the night. I bet the boys got away with armfuls of sugary snakes, or whatever it is they are eating these days. I used to think Afghan hounds looked stupid with their big, geeky legs and long, blond hair till I found out they were perfect for their job. Anyway, in a round about way I'm saying that even though the boys sometimes look a bit like a pack of hounds, they have way more talent than that.

Once back in the school building, they looked more of a unit again: walking the corridors automatically, fanning out a bit as they pass through the diner to fill the emptiness. Schools feel weird at night with no kids in them. Unnatural. You can feel the presence of kids everywhere but there aren't any. The echoey darkness and occasional soft glow of emergency lights doesn't help with the spookiness.

"Let's not piss about," said Travis loudly to fill some silence. He was impatient to be done with it.

"Why, you got something goin' on later?" Christie is up for a wind-up.

"So what if I have?" Has anyone else noticed the change in Travis these past few days? Like part of him has come home from the war and is ready for peace. The fact that he's been seen around a lot recently with that cute new girl in the sixth form has probably got something to do with it. She's got stars-of-a-thousand-skies eyes and a voice like melted chocolate. Her parents must be going out of their minds.

Greg and Billy were walking together, talking in low voices. They are very different, but they understand each other's strengths and weaknesses. Like they've got used to all the things they might not really like or dislike about each other. It makes them seem more grown up the way they get on.

Martin was hoovering up the corridor like a racehorse on the way to the starting line. Like his evening personality was too big for the school. Like he needed it wide open to have space for his mood. He was using the shadows as stepping stones to avoid the cameras. Tunes in one ear, alert in the other. He's one of those who knows how the best plans goes.

A couple of years ago, if the boys had got into school at night, they would have behaved very differently: leaving a trail of destruction as they got what they could out of the entertainment. Maybe they just weren't in the mood. Maybe having the keys took the 'one time excitement' out of it.

They headed straight for the caretaker's office. Without really discussing it, all were anxious to get the job done. As Greg said on the way in, it was lucky they hadn't been nailed for the keys already, but it meant that the CCTV hadn't been checked yet.

The caretaker's office was warm with the glow from the ranks of screens. Piles of paper and memos lay in drifts on the desk. A large photo of an owl was glaring down on them from the shelf with a look of late-night disapproval, like a woken parent. Greg found himself thinking that the screens looked like those documentaries you see where they film the Titanic at the bottom of the sea.

Christie and Travis set about the task of finding and deleting the evidence while Billy explored the potential of the desk drawers. The different cameras were only numbered and it was proving more difficult than they thought to find what they wanted to delete. So much for four years of Information Technology lessons, but they can seem like a computer game in themselves sometimes. Trying to get on 'Vietcong' for long enough to kill each other without being collared by a teacher is enough of a high level challenge – never mind navigating your way through the school's internet blocking systems.

Greg joined in and started reorganizing the method of attack, but they still couldn't find Christie's key-stealing Oscar performance.

Billy was having more success with the drawers. He soon discovered some user guides for the system, which were passed on to Greg pretty quickly at the sight of all that small print, putting Greg in charge of the operation for a while.

I suppose it's one of the reasons why they are my favourites, that there are so many natural leaders in one gang. It makes a rare kind of team. It's also what makes a lot of people feel intimidated by them; you can't use the usual 'deal with the leader and you've dealt with them all' technique that teachers use on most gangs. You have to earn them all. Somehow it makes their good opinion worth having.

No-one had noticed that Martin had slipped out till he came bursting back in smiling.

"Did that help?" he asked.

"What, you fucking off when we're trying to get this sorted?" says Billy, "how is that supposed to help??"

"Didn't you see me jumpin' up an down like an idiot?" Martin seemed a bit disappointed. "I've been up to M6 an' you know what, that caretaker's still in there! I heard him movin' about. Explains why we didn't get busted for the keys yet anyway."

"We weren't going to get busted anyway," said Travis, "I've been watching the screens the whole time and I didn't see Martin. That camera doesn't work. It's frozen. That's why we can't find it to delete it."

"Well it worked this afternoon or we wouldn't have got the keys," said Billy, "although this might explain why the caretaker didn't get out!" and he pulled a mobile phone out of the desk drawer. "Should've kept it in his pocket!"

The boys pretty much knew that the caretaker's phone was likely to spend the next part of its life in Billy's pocket, but so what. It wasn't really the issue now.

Martin ran off again to the Maths corridor, and they made sure the M6 camera didn't work. Things in school break all the time, but it's cool when they do it conveniently.

They didn't push their luck by giving in to the temptation of winding up the caretaker though. It was pretty amazing that he'd been stuck in there so long anyway. How did it happen? Still, the dignity of a high school caretaker is a delicate thing. It might have been hard for him to have to knock and get some passing Year Seven to go for help. And given the day he'd been having there was probably some attraction in having just one corner of a quiet classroom to deal with for a while. It saved the boys a job anyway and things started to get a bit more entertaining when Billy pulled out his latest find – a tape marked 'Greatest Hits'. They loaded it in and settled down with everything edible the office contained, to watch the highlights.

It was quite a collection, as you would expect from school. There was some Year Ten doing a ridiculous dance number down a corridor (pretty funny though…), there were a couple of fairly heavy fights cut from different cameras, even some junior girls flashing at some builders (but you couldn't really see anything). There were two male teachers tumbling out of what looked like the theatre doors wearing wigs and dresses. Billy himself along with a very wound-up Greg featured too. There was a smoke bomb from a few years ago. The camera got it really well from ignition to explosion, and even though the boys laughed at the kid who nearly walked right past it, and just pulled back through the door in time, they were quietly shocked at the near miss he'd had. Well you've got to laugh when you're at school.

For a while they were all relaxed, looking like those puppies in '101 Dalmatians' who sat all evening in the firelight at Cruella DeVil's fur-factory watching TV. (But without the spots obviously!)

Greg started to lose interest and went back to the system computer.

"Sez here you can set up a web link for viewing the CCTV over the internet," he said. "Might as well give it a go, it could come in useful sometime to be able to hack it."

Travis started to get involved again, watching Greg work through the activation; his hazel eyes narrowed with concentration.

"What the fuck was that?" shouted Christie all of a sudden, and all of a sudden everyone was half way to their feet and staring at a screen on the second row. "There was something there!" Christie was looking quite serious, but they'd had a Christie wind-up or two in the past.

"Yeah right," comes back Billy, lounging back again in the comfiest chair, stretching his legs out, taking up some space. "When we've just been watching the ghost clips. As if!" but before he could continue, he caught the look on Martin's face and his eyes shot back to the screens. They all saw it this time, something had definitely moved past the camera, something quite big too.

There was a moment of silence. Everyone was very still, staring at the camera. Greg was looking up from the desk, the mouse frozen in his hand, mouth slightly open, intent on the screens. They seemed to be aware all at once of themselves in a tiny, lighted space in the middle of a huge dark building. The moment held its breath until the screens started to stir into life again. Large dark figures were moving around the building. It was unclear how many there were as they passed through the screens but it was clear they were headed this way. And whoever they were, the boys didn't want to find out.

The caretaker's office became a flurry of movement as the boys cleared out of it for the second time that day. The door had nearly finished shutting itself when Greg suddenly ducked back in, clicked 'apply' on the computer screen and then disappeared out again...

*** 

*By this point in the story our lessons were going pretty well. The boys didn't come into the room like it was a ring any more anyway. They'd have a chat, settle down, borrow pens. I looked forward to our lessons, and I missed the boys on the days they weren't there. There was still a lot of swearing but I'd decided on balance to ignore that for a while. I wanted them to discuss things, and express their opinions, so it seemed a bit counter-productive to stop them at every F. I wanted to send out a friendly message that I was interested in what they'd got to say by letting them say it how they wanted. Once you turn swearing into a bit of a treat, it's bound to lose its ghetto-chic pretty quickly and wear off.*

*I'd more or less got over my fear that they might just decide to break into the school after I'd gone and put the idea out there. I'd even made them a reading exercise in the form of a mock legal declaration which they had all signed to say they would not, among other things, break into the school. I had no idea then of course, that this declaration would be held up in a courtroom one day by a snowy-cuffed barrister with his own lectern, as evidence that I had secretly intended to publish the story all along and had tried to cover myself with this attempt at creating a legal document, but it's weird making up a story about the building you are in and the people there with you. Real and imagined things start to overlap at the edges in your head. Especially when the story is still going on. You know what is real and what is made up of course, but having both existing in the same space kind of adds a new dimension to everything. Like your real self and your anti-matter self go to the same school but they don't hang out together. Like they walk through each other in the corridors.*

*Some things you make up actually happen after a while, because of the flow of the patterns of a system in a building. Or because of the magic of stories. It makes it harder to explain how you made it all up to a disciplinary panel that's for sure.*

*We talked a bit about this kid Daniel Beaver one time. He was one of those quiet skinny boys who you always see on their own. His hair was darker than it should be. His face was paler than it should be. He was one of those kids who never wanted to go home at the end of school. And he looked pretty miserable at school. He'd hang about the corridors as the building emptied, till only the staff were left, and the cleaners started to arrive. No-one ever really noticed him leaving. Then one day he didn't turn up at home, and his parents rang the school. He wasn't there either. The police were called after a few more hours, and then the search began. Nothing was heard about Daniel Beaver. He'd just disappeared.*

*Two months later there was a break-in at the school.*

*I swear you could almost stroke the silence in the room as the boys listened. They get so into a story – when it's not read from a book of course.*

*No-one could work out how the intruders had got in, or where they had got in, but signs of a break-in were found by the caretaker the next morning.*

*"What sort of signs?" Travis is sitting with both feet up on the desk, rocked back, need I say. He's dyed his hair again – a dark red this time.*

*They'd all gone so quiet it made me jump when he said it. I was really into the Daniel Beaver story.*

*"What sort of signs? Well. Doors open that had been left closed, you know, furniture moved, and muffin wrappers on the floor!"*

*"Fucking muffin wrappers!? What's that got to do with anything?"*

*(Maybe I went a bit far with the muffin wrappers)*

*Anyway a few weeks after that, some teachers started to complain that they heard noises like some animal was living in the ceiling, and the caretaker launched a search of the building, and down in the old boiler room they found this kind of nest made out of bits of blanket and old PE Kits.*

*The caretaker set up watch to see what the nest belonged to. It was Daniel Beaver. Turns out his parents were violent, and he was scared to go home, and one day he just hid in the building and never dared come out again. Which explained the muffin wrappers – because all he'd had to live on were the things in the bins, so he used to go to the big one by the diner door at night and scavenge for muffins. Poor boy.*

*"What the fuck happened to him when they found him?" demands Billy. Billy and his way of making a question sound a bit like an order. It's the swagger that gets you.*

*Poor Daniel had to be taken straight to the hospital to be put on vitamin drips and stuff, because even though a diet of muffins sounds quite nice, it doesn't give you what your body needs.*

*"I know what my body needs!" Ha Ha Billy!*

*Then he had to go to all these psychiatrists and things because of the trauma he had suffered hiding in the school. Hearing life go on. He must have been in a real state ...*

*"I didn't mean that," Billy cut in, "I meant what punishment did he get when they caught him?"*

*Well there was none. He'd had a terrible ordeal. I don't know if he went back to his parents or not.*

*Our discussion continued on, until it got as far as whether Daniel had spied on the girls' changing rooms from the ceiling panels or not.*

*"As if he didn't! What would you do if you were Daniel Beaver and you'd been there for months, without a TV even?"*

*It's an angle on Daniel Beaver I wouldn't have thought of myself, but I'm not a teenage boy am I, so it wouldn't enter my head every three seconds, or whatever the statistics say about boys and sex.*

*Then Martin took out a headphone, and busted me on my story. He sits so smalled up in the corner most of the time, and it's like when he pulls out the headphones, he's pulling out the cord in one of those self-inflating life-jackets, and he suddenly becomes much larger in the room. Most of him is usually miles away in his music. You can almost hear the 'whoosh' when he comes back from there. He turns to the others,*

*"She's totally taking the piss! There's no such person as Daniel Beaver is there?"*

*I'm trying not to smile the wrong smile now. Trying to tell them how Katie and Becca were crying when they saw poor Daniel being carried out to the ambulance, and how they couldn't bear the thought of him under the floor, silently listening to the happy children in the classrooms ... Katie with her hair like Rapunzel, and Becca with her hair like Snow White..*

*"Yeah but you're still totally lying!"*

*Martin who's never sure of anything in a classroom, except that he doesn't really want to be there, is totally sure about this one. We were all laughing by then. I had been well and truly busted. He said home couldn't be so bad that anyone would want to spend the rest of their miserable life in school for fuck's sake! Day and night.*

*"Whatever you say about the fucking muffins – it isn't worth it!" HA!*

*They are so perceptive when it comes to such things. I'd had the Daniel Beaver story going for years without being rumbled till I told them. Daniel had run and run. I once overheard a member of staff talking about him in the staffroom, saying it was lucky the press didn't get hold of it at the time and wondering how the poor kid was doing now. The more years I told the Daniel Beaver story, the more I learned about it myself. Kids who'd seen him being put in the ambulance. Kids who'd seen him in the local supermarket, looking lonely, hiding behind his fringe, and who wished they'd talked to him and cheered him up a bit. When I was suspended from duty, the parents of all students in this story were contacted. As he was a named child, some secretary probably had to go through the hassle of typing a letter to Daniel's parents before realising he wasn't on the system. I know my union rep had him on his list of children involved. In fact when I explained about the creative nature of Daniel to my solicitor, his daughter who overheard us was outraged, having been taught by me at school and having been a long-time Daniel-pittier with the rest of her class. HA! She had no idea I'd made him up.*

*Anyway, I went to make the boys tea in the end. Well, we were having a good time, and behaving is thirsty work sometimes. I was thinking about it on the way to the office kitchen. We'd had a good chat, whether Daniel Beaver was real or not, because there are Daniel Beavers everywhere. I love that about stories.*

*They remind you of life. They can happen anywhere. Anything can happen. And they can start and end at any time.*

*Then I got back with the tea to an empty classroom. They'd done one. The weasels.*

*Still, it can take just a bit longer than however long you've got to learn that respect isn't something you get, it's something you give.*

## The Legal Declaration

*I do solemnly swear that the content of this story is purely fictional and that I will not attempt to break in to the school under any circumstances, or poor old Miss Rusty will surely get the sack.*

*I would also like to donate ten percent of my future earnings to keep my beloved English teacher in hot chocolate in her old age.*

*My suggestion for the title of the book is ............*
*..................................................*

*signed ...........*

*Date ...............*

*Tag (optional) ........................................*

*A reading exercise*
*March 2008*

# Stop! Don't read this!
## Chapter 4

It was weird pitching up at school the next morning, like when you find yourself in a place you think you once dreamed about. (or 'nightmared' about more like, if 'nightmared' was a word). It looked as if nothing had happened. Same old, same old school, with a bell that you hear in your bloodstream, and routes you just take without thinking about it.

The boys met somewhere between the light-up, and the dock-out, of a little pre-school number, and mulled over the chances of trouble. Talking in low, sideways voices on the way in. There were only a few late stragglers around now, and they mostly slowed down or sped up to keep out of the way of the boys.

"It's a good job we know where the cameras are," Greg was saying. "Don't think we'd be identifiable anyway."

They'd made it out of school the night before without being seen, but as they'd run low round the shadowy back of the maths block, Travis had remembered the keys, right back at square one in the caretaker's office. Too late to do anything about that. Let it go.

"Who were they though?" Billy asked as they headed into school for registration, along the front drive and in up the steps. No-one had an answer for that one, so no-one said much as they went along the main corridor. They were thinking back to the figures on the screens: big guys, with unclear faces. Moving through the building like it was their own.

The school day wore on as school days do, with its occasional highs … (well it was Friday =)

Not much was heard about the caretaker being locked in. They asked around a bit at break, and sent it through the network, but nothing came back. As Travis suggested, the trail probably went dry when they discovered the M6 camera had stopped working. GdGd. All the same, the boys kept a low profile so as not to attract unnecessary attention from staff. By the end of lunchtime it started to seem weird that there was no news of a break in. What were those guys doing in school in the middle of the night if they weren't nicking something? None of them could shake the strange feeling that they had been trespassed on. I mean it's one thing abusing your own school, but just let anyone else try it! It's a funny one. You have to be part of it, to have the right to diss it.

On the way to period five, Martin suggested that if they logged on to the web link (remember – the one set up just in time the night before by the quick-witted super-hero Greg Bratley), they might be able to find out what was actually going on.

"When are we gonna do that?" Christie wants to know.

"We could get Miss Rusty to make us tea in English and go on the computer while she's gone. She'll do it if she thinks it'll get some work out of us." Good idea Travis.

Maybe the boys thought for a moment how lucky they were to have such an amazing teacher who was willing to go out the door, through the double doors, across the corridor, through more double doors, into the icy quad with the wind howling and rain lashing around, and in through the next double doors, and along past the diner, and up the History staircase, and into the staffroom, through two more doors, and over to where the PE staff sit, to 'rob' their teabags, and over to the Pupil Support office, to 'rob' their sugar, and then to carry all the tea back down again without spilling it …

Or maybe they just thought that all that tea-making hassle would buy them plenty of time to get on the staff computer and see what they could find out about last night's intruders. And with the added bonus of a cup of tea at the end of it of course :D

I don't know. A while ago they would have just thought about what was in it for themselves, but the boys really are growing up these days. It gets harder and harder to see them just as kids. Well if you think about it, kids have pretty intense lives. They are changing all the time. No wonder they look at teachers like they do, when they're banging on about their French homework being late, and how-important-it-is to hand things in on time. Jee-sus. Sometimes life, and the need to hand in your French homework, are completely incompatible universes.

*In the governors' disciplinary hearing to which I was subjected, this section of the story was included in the many examples of ways in which I fell below the professional standards expected of a teacher. Can you believe it – stealing 'items of food' from other members of staff to give to students. In a story! I'm lucky I escaped jail.*

*I remember wondering how many meetings it had taken to decide on 'items of food' as the most appropriate way of summarising 'teabags and sugar'. Sometimes Professional Standards and the need to just be a real person are completely incompatible universes too.*

Anyway, while The Wonderful Teacher was out on the Tea Marathon, Greg got on to the web link and soon they were all crowded round the now familiar CCTV interface. They scanned it back to the night before, and ended up looking at the unknown figures, moving about the dark school corridors.

Just sitting in classrooms as usual in broad daylight, with the hum of people everywhere, it had been hard to see last night as real. The corridors, where the boys themselves liked to create a scary presence, had shown no sign of the strangers who'd been there last night. Now that they were looking at the cameras, it started to bring the whole thing back to life. There seemed to be three, possibly four of them: big, jaily looking guys with hard faces. Totally unfamiliar.

"Looks like whatever they nicked is in them," said Christie as they finally caught a shot of three of the men carrying large white cases that might have been made of polystyrene. "Projectors maybe?"

They watched the clip again in case they had missed something. Billy started to get twitchy, and started telling Christie go and watch the door. Then Travis pointed out that the footage of the white boxes was the earliest bit when the intruders had just got in.

"It's something they brought in with them then," Martin added. "Fuck knows what though."

Greg kept working through the cameras to see if they could find out anything else. He was getting quite good with the software. All that 'Vietcong' training in illegitimate IT lesson moments was paying off. It's that way you sometimes get an education, in spite of your education. They all watched intently, trying to make some sense out of it. The room was quiet apart from the occasional thud, or raised voice, through the wall from L12.

"Just go back to that one before," said Travis, and they waited while the image loaded. They all saw it this time. One of the intruders entered the screen. His face was set grim, and there was a dangerous kind of look about him. Like you wouldn't pick him to ask if he'd go into the off-licence for you. Like you wouldn't want to catch his eye on a Saturday night in the square. He was carrying a box, easily, and gave the impression that if someone else was holding it, the box would have looked much bigger and heavier. Crossing the camera, he seemed to just disappear as he walked past a pillar. He never came out the other side.

"Where is that?" Christie asked. But none of them could place it. They continued to watch the camera until they'd seen three men pass by the pillar and disappear in the same spot. Strange indeed. The corridor in the shot was pretty dark, but not dark enough to miss anyone walking past.

"We should find out where that camera is," said Greg. "It's annoying me now".

"Well there's one way to sort that," said Martin. "It'll have to be now though. It'll be too busy to see when the bell goes."

Greg reset the camera to current time, to watch as the others piled out of the door. They'd been still for more than long enough, and the run began.

Travis went via the staffroom to delay the tea-making, Martin took the Science Block, Maths and Humanities, Billy had English and PE and Tech, Christie had the rest. They were hardly getting any speed up before Greg called Martin's phone.

"Just go back the way you came, but slowly," said Greg and Martin headed back down the corridor. He saw the pillar before Greg had time to say "Stop!" and he saw the cleaners' cupboard that was hidden from the camera behind it.

Christie and Billy turned up, breathing harder from a circuit of the building. Martin tried the door handle. Unlocked. The others followed him inside. With the door pulled shut behind them, it took a while for their eyes to get used to the gloomy light.

It was a typical cleaners' cupboard: bigger than you would have expected, with a sink in one corner and the smell of that bubblegum floor cleaner they always use in schools (as if that would improve the smell of the place). There were mops in the corner, and buckets stacked up, and bottles of detergent. No white boxes.

"Why would they all come in here though?" Billy wants to know. "Why this shithole?" He kicked the stack of mop buckets and they went all over the place, rolling around, and taking up quite a lot of space in their unstacked state. Christie fell over one in the half light, and swore as he hit a shelf on the way to the floor. Greg and Travis arrived just as the bell went and the corridors began to flood, pulling the door shut behind them, and telling some nosey kid to fuck off, as Billy tried to shove a bucket on Christie's head.

"Gerroff!" said Christie in a muffled (bucket-covered) voice. "Check this out! I think I've found something".

Billy surrendered the bucket as his curiosity got the better of him, and they all squatted down to see what Christie had found. The floor was not a solid floor and if you looked as closely as Christie had done when his head hit it, you could see the faint outline of a trapdoor. Quite a big trapdoor.

They looked at it for a moment. No one said a word. Then the old gang telepathy kicked in again. Billy, Christie, and Greg moved back clearing the buckets and bottles out of the way, Travis reached in his pocket, got out his pride-and-joy personalized zippo, and lit it above the trapdoor while Martin prised it open at one corner with a key.

It swung up easily though it wasn't particularly light, and rested back against the wall. The little pool of yellow cast by Travis' lighter didn't show much. Martin went first, and one by one the boys disappeared from view down the hole.

* * *

*It's all been said before about teenagers and technology, but we are still not getting their level. All we actually get is that we just don't get it, and still we try to impose an order on it all.*

*Take 'Mosquito' as a simple example, that high pitched tone adopted in shopping malls to deter teenagers from hanging around. While the adults were still locked in debate about whether it was morally right to use it on young people, some of those young people already had the sound as a ringtone because their teachers couldn't hear it. I value that kind of creativity. It's like a martial art, using the attack of your opponent as power for yourself. Well, kids don't really have any power do they, so I suppose they often have to re-use someone else's.*

*When I was suspended, the kids held a demonstration at the school: police cars, press, the works. They organised it overnight via social networking. Christie called me from the scene and left a message on my phone. It said, "Listen to this Miss!" and he held up his phone so I could hear the buzz. I have to admit it was awesome, listening to that noise of kids. It took me right back to my school somehow. My last live memory of the job. Not long after the phone call, photos and links to video clips of hundreds of kids in the demonstration, began dropping in my inbox. Some thoughtful child sent me a shot of the crowd from my old classroom window, so that I could pretend I was looking on from there. There were some from our kids, and some from kids at other schools who were following the demonstration from their own IT lessons, and receiving regular updates via mobile link-up from our school front field. Kids I'd never even met.*

*I know they should have been doing their schoolwork, but let's not forget that some of our best memories come from rare moments when we weren't doing quite what we were supposed to be doing. Teenagers and communication technology. I actually can't wait to see what this generation do with the adult world when they inherit it. We think we are advanced with our endless emails: a quaint, rustic form of communication which kids abandoned years ago.*

*I marvel at what it must be like growing up potentially having everyone you know, anywhere in the world, online in your bedroom throughout your life. Kids are so connected. It gives them such an unquantifiable access to support that they have normalised discord and public humiliations in a way we can't comprehend, to the extent where they engage regularly in frank group discussion with their enemies on sites like Formspring. They are also remarkably savvy about who they give access to and how they share information. I grew up before the internet so I couldn't imagine being able to bear that feeling of exposure. I think the idea of it makes us old people feel vulnerable, because online consciousness has moved beyond our psychological horizons. Before the advent of the internet, being a kid was a way more isolated experience. Once you were in your room you were on your own.*

*We have to get over our fear of the internet. Adults who grew up before it existed experience a loss of control similar to growing up in the village you were born in and being dropped in Brooklyn in the middle of the night, without currency or even a subway map. Young people are not afraid of the internet. It's not a strange city to them. They know how to get around, where the good bits are and which streets to avoid after midnight. They can find their friends wherever they are, they know who to smile at and who will smile back and why. They've outgrown our warnings of Stranger Danger, and it's time to trust the young to show us round.*

*I went through days of disciplinary proceedings over the issue of this story and its brief advent on the internet. It was regarded as 'a serious breach of data protection and human rights issues' which put all the students named in the story at risk. From start to finish, neither the accusers nor myself really had any idea what that meant or how they were at risk and none of us do to this day – but it sounded impressive to all of us.*

*Nowadays, when some poor nice girl gets caught with some guy round the back of the Co-op, the photo flashes from phone to phone by Sunday morning, and by Monday they have to face school. I always wondered how they cope with it. You'd think they'd never live it down. Then when the papers got hold of my story it didn't take long before my picture went half way round the world with headlines about my pupil sex fantasies, and I came to realise how quickly your media self and your real self separate. Everyone I ever knew heard about it. I may as well have been caught round the back of the Co-op myself.*

*I must apologise for that ghastly image.*

*Since I got sacked I have spoken to some of the kids who were involved in the demonstration. They found it empowering. It wasn't the kind of empowerment connected with winning or losing. It was a pride in organising themselves and in expressing their feelings. I got the impression in the Disciplinary Hearing, that the support of pupils and parents rather angered the panel, and it has been suggested that without it the process might have been less severe. I was found guilty of bringing the school into disrepute for all the publicity, and of demeaning pupils and parents among various other things. All I can say to that really is that the support of the community kept me from losing heart, kept me from being disappeared, and helped me keep sight of what pupils and parents actually value in teachers. When push comes to shove (and I think it's fair to say we were probably well past shove by the time the hearing took place) I'd have to choose to keep my heart over my job. Those kids gave me a hell of a send off, and I honour them for that. But there are tons of things I honour them for, the little rascals!*

# Jago

Jago's been tired for weeks, which feel like years.

It's that kind of tired where you can't be bothered to think very long about anything much.

And everything's noisy.

Jago never knows if he's fallen asleep at night and when he wakes up it feels like he was never asleep.

He could do without the hassle.

He's resting his chin on his hands and looking up. Listening to Mr Blero talking about his cat. He's telling them how he got it as a scraggy kitten and really looked after it. Then he's telling them he took it to the vets to 'get done' and that he'll never forget the way the cat looked at him when it came back from the vets with its balls chopped off. Blero says the cat totally knew it was his fault.

It's peaceful and warm and everyone is listening. Not because it is particularly exciting, old Blero's story about the cat, but he gets into 'rambling mode' and somehow there is often a kind of point. Like he tells you a story about three strawberries in a row behind the glass of a slot machine, and then your brain kind of makes the winnings come out at the bottom. That kind of a point.

Even though he can't actually see them from where he is, Jago knows that Aaron is sitting near Beth and there is a half-finished note to her under his hand. Beth isn't even waiting to reply to the note because for them, like everyone else in the room, everything is suddenly about Mr. Blero's cat. Soon there'll be an opportunity for relating their own pet-stories. Surprise puppy experiences, lost puppy experiences, always wanted a dog experiences.

Someone is already wondering if it's safe to tell about when they ran down the stairs and stomped on one of the kittens by accident. Someone else is trying not to think about the time when they tortured a hamster.

Memories of old dogs being put to sleep, and seeing rock-solid dads brushing tears away, are escaping to the fronts of minds.

A goldfish bobs up to lie stiff on the surface, with one eye out of the water. Haydn tries to explain how when he was a kid and his goldfish died, that's when he realised it's the way they move that makes goldfish beautiful, not the gold.

Some girl flips over her planner to reveal a sellotaped picture of a gorgeous Siamese in front of a gas fire. A boy remembers a party where his older brother gave the dog blowbacks to see if it liked getting stoned. It didn't, so they gave it some beer to take its mind off things. It didn't seem to care about anything after that, but it was ecstatic when the parents got home the next day to a suspiciously tidy house.

Jago finds himself thinking that it's wild how many experiences one cat story can trigger in a group of thirty kids. This is one of those lessons he still feels part of, unlike others where he feels like he has fallen between the tracks. It's even wilder that by the time the bell goes and they've all been shared, everyone somehow knows more about 'Poems From Other Cultures' than they did at the start. Fucking awesome.

It's History next, and Jago imagines the scene: same kids, different roles, and a teacher who will spoon-feed them the horrors of war. Then with no sense of irony at all, she'll find out that they haven't done their tests properly, and line them up against the wall to be shot.

He heads into the corridor where all calm is washed away and the tiredness hits him again. People say teenagers need a lot of sleep because of all the growing they are doing. But what about the things that really age you? The things that happen that make it fucking ridiculous pretending to still feel twelve years old. Sometimes you are forced to get older all of a sudden and no-one seems to understand how tiring that is. Except maybe those people you hear about who've been in comas for ten years, and they wake up to a world that's not the same any more, and there's no going back. They must feel knackered!

Jago is walking behind Maddy. She used to walk behind him, winding him up like girls do, with the kind of hair that showed how late she got up. Now she has curves, and long beach-blond clayed tousled locks, and moves with a swing in her hips and just a bit of lace showing.

She is texting as she walks, like she needs technology to transport her out of her age group.

As he passes 'the Ghetto', Jago slows up to see if the boys are still there. So does Maddy. There's only Miss Rusty, with her back turned, cleaning the board. He gets the feeling she's not up for visitors and carries on. He would have liked a chat with Travis on the way to period 6. Jago finds that more and more he feels at home with the older boys. He's been running both sides for a while, but this one is winning. Somehow their chaos gives him peace. It's not as noisy as the rest.

Jago had a food fight with Maddy in Year 7, back when she used to wind him up. He remembers watching Maddy, arguing back while Mr Praznik gave her a detention. She was standing defiant, with spaghetti hoops splattered across her cleavage. Happy Days!

Jago passed right by the cleaners' cupboard on the way to History. It was in the corridor where Travis had a fight last year with his now ex-best friend. It was fierce to the end. And it made strangers out of them. It's worse fighting people you know. You think you're really close to someone, and then suddenly you are miles apart … unlike Travis and Jago, who were not remotely miles apart, when Jago passed right by the cleaners' cupboard on the way to History.

It really wasn't a very exciting looking cleaners' cupboard.

* * *

*This bit is a bit soft so feel free to skip to the next chapter. I wouldn't blame you. It's only like going to get popcorn at the cinema ...*

*I was just going to say – How lovely is it to be in a classroom where your teacher loves you. And how much you can say and feel when you know someone is interested in your opinion. How much stronger do you feel when you know someone cares about you. How funny are you when you know you can make people laugh.*

*When I was at university I was supposed to be studying languages, so I went to all the psychology lectures instead. That was just my way of rebelling I suppose. Sounds tragic I know, but I learned some cool stuff. Like I learned that it doesn't really matter what you are learning, so long as you are learning something. And I learned about Harlow and Suomi. They were scientists who did experiments with monkeys. They'd get a new born baby monkey and put it in a cage with a choice of two mothers. One mother was a tube of wire with monkey milk on tap. The other was furry and had a face but no food. Harlow and Suomi proved that the baby monkeys choose the furry-faced mother over one that will feed them. How gutting is that!*

*When I've told children about this experiment in class, and showed them a picture of the baby monkey hanging on to the dummy mum, I can feel their spirits creep forward like I'm providing food and furriness. It's lovely when that happens. A kind of peace comes over us all and a kind of glow comes off the kids. It's the same when I read this story with my boys.*

*Kids understand the value of love and comfort, because nothing helps them more. The baby monkey is a lesson which confirms what they already know. It shows them that adults don't always*

79

*have as much faith as children, and that the adult world wants funky scientific monkey proof to show what children need.*

*I still think the Harlow and Suomi experiment is beautiful. The yellow cloth mother with the red plastic eyes is like a Madonna to me. She confirms that even in the most institutional environment like a science lab, love is the business. That is about as close as I like to get to a religious experience.*

*I brought Harlow and Suomi up in my Disciplinary Hearing, but they said my evidence was vexatious. I got a kind message while I was suspended from some guy in the technology department, offering to build me a nice big cross on the front field. The whole thing certainly felt like a crucifixion to me. That's definitely going one religious experience too far for anyone.*

# Stop! Don't read this!
## Chapter 5
## The Void

As I imagine it now, the boys disappearing through that trapdoor one by one, it makes me think of how it will be when they leave school. Disappearing one by one into the unknown.

Have you ever noticed how much you can tell from looking at the back of someone you know? Like what kind of mood they are in, or things they usually hide better from the front. The boys specialize in mass departures as I said before, so I've had plenty of opportunities to study them from the back (I was going to say 'analyse', but you can't say a word that has 'anal' in it when you are talking about the backs of your students. Jee-sus!).

You get good at spotting your favourites in a crowd as well. Like people who look at the stars always have a favourite star or constellation that they look for to fix themselves. You never know when you might need it. Then one day you'll go to somewhere on the other side of the planet, and the sky will show you how far you have come. Like I stood on a hill once in Hong Kong, amazed that the moon looks like a smile from over there. You may as well see for yourself that the world isn't flat. Why take it from anybody else?

Anyway, with this crew it is really obvious to see from behind that they are a close unit on the outside, but their internal worlds are worlds apart. If I was trying to be poetic, I'd say they're like a group of islands that are close enough together to suffer the same weather. I know, I should quit trying to be poetic and get back to the action.

As I was saying, seeing it in my mind's eye, the boys disappearing one by one through that trapdoor, is like the last scene from some old Russian play called 'The End of Schoolski' or something. It makes me start stressing about whether I've really taught them anything useful for the world out there while I've had them. I haven't even taught them the Crosswinds Rule, and the Crosswinds Rule is one of the best rules around. It's amazing how in the modern world no-one knows it except sailors.

Just in case you are wanting to exchange ignorance for knowledge on the whole Crosswinds Rule thing – stand with your back to the wind, watch which way the clouds are moving (they are always moving by the way!) If they are moving from left to right, the weather will get worse. Good to know.

So they disappeared down the hatch. Travis was last, being a pretty obvious choice for holding the trapdoor up for the rest. Martin had the lighter poised somewhere around what seemed like it might be about half way down the dusty staircase. The flame cast a small, flickery pool of light quite bravely for a bit, before it guttered out. The darkness smelled warm and uninhabited. The darkness felt somehow very spacious.

Greg and Billy were both reaching for their phones to create a bit of light, when they heard a noise above. Someone was opening the cupboard door.

Travis lowered the trapdoor over them as quickly and quietly as possible. The only shaft of dim light from the top of the steps folded up like a fan till it was just a thin white line in the darkness. Then it vanished with a sharp click as whoever it was that had just come in to the cleaners' cupboard, waded through the buckets, and stood on the trapdoor.

There was no time to work out whether whoever it was up there knew about the trapdoor or not. Travis had to jump back to avoid losing a few fingers as it snapped shut. He lost his footing in the darkness, and fell backwards through something that felt like Christie, and something a bit more resistant which was probably Billy, before knocking Greg and Martin down ahead of him.

It was a pity the Health and Safety inspector hadn't been given the chance to admire this bit of the school, because there didn't seem to be any rails or banisters or useful things like that, so it was pretty much free-fall till they hit the uneven floor below. Just a bit more than far enough to get some good bruises and scuffs. No-one had made a sound as they fell.

There's something very disorientating about falling quietly in complete darkness. They lay still where they landed for a minute, listening for sounds from above, making a mental note of what hurt.

Have you ever had that experience of waking up at night thinking you are in your own room, and then realising that something doesn't feel right? And it takes you a while to remember you're at Mitch's house or somewhere. It's a weird one. Your senses start to tingle but it's usually over almost before you know it, as your eyes get used to the dark and you start to see the wardrobe emerging, and a vague square of window. Down there in the darkness, the darkness just went on. Velvety and suffocating. As the seconds ticked by, it wasn't really clear whether it was a relief or a shame that the trapdoor didn't open to reveal an angry teacher. They got to their feet.

Still no-one had spoken. Now that there was suddenly no sound but their own shifting about, they became aware of how much noise school usually makes. It was as if it had just disappeared.

Greg was feeling around for his phone which he'd dropped on the way down.

It would be discovered years later by a demolition company guy. Long, long years after its battery had died, taking with it the glow of a short message which had come through as it was falling, telling of undying love, from a certain pretty year 8…

*It was time for an assessment. I was feeling unusually confident about even suggesting it as our lessons hadn't been going too badly recently. I'd dare to say the boys looked forward to them, but I was keeping up the supply of tea and treats because, let's face it, sometimes you need a good excuse to look forward to a lesson. Progress was still hampered by exclusions and the usual institutional crap, but you know, no-one's got a magic wand or anything.*

*Martin and Christie were suspended from lessons. They were not allowed to return to class that week. I sent a message to the office saying that they were supposed to be writing an assessment, and suggesting that this would increase their punishment, but it made no difference. They were to stay outside the Headteacher's office, on Death Row till the end of the school week.*

*"So why are they excluded?" I make the mistake of asking.*

*Greg takes up the story and tells it greg-stylee..*

*"There's this guy in town, a real scrote. He just hangs round pissed an' all that, an' scrounging money off anyone he can. He's like in his forties or something. You'd feel a bit sorry for him if he wasn't such a sad bastard. He's got kids an' all, an' he's begging for beers off teenagers in the street every day. Fucking pathetic. We wind him up a bit sometimes, well it serves him right really. Like we make him do dances an' shit like that for a beer, or half a beer, or whatever. One time we got him to eat a piece of dog shit off the street for a can! It was disgusting! He did it though! Scratty bastard! Anyway a couple of days ago, we were out of school at lunchtime, an' we saw him get hold of this kid and start smacking him around for no reason. We were just walking past and he starts giving it 'whatTheFuckArYouLookinAt?' an' all that. We went to get some food an' we saw him again on*

*the way back; bottle in his hand, fucking looking at us. Then he starts again, mouthing off an' we just jumped him. Anyway, one of the neighbours phoned school an' complained an' they must have described Christie an' Martin coz they got busted for it. Typical. No-one is interested in the fact that he's smacking kids around. He's a total waste of space!"*

*How could it not mess with my head really. I have a full-sized class of Year Tens on my timetable who are studying 'Oliver Twist'. I have them every week, the lesson before these guys. They are a wonderful class with their own share of personalities, and they are writing these amazing essays about the terrible times Charles fucking Dickens was trying to change. The same school, two lessons apart, one class are writing about the need for society to give kids a fair chance in the 1830s, and the other class are living it in 2008.*

*So we are down to three on assessment day.*

***Choose a character from the first five chapters. Describe them and their role in the story.***

*Quiet sort of falls and they start the task. I settle down at my desk at the front to pretend I am working and I watch them, thinking about their life experiences which are so far from mine.*

*Billy is a bit slower to start, he pops his head up at the slightest noise or movement just in case there is going to be a good distraction, but there isn't one really, and pretty soon he is working, or looking like he is working.*

*It's a shame there aren't many moments when they are all so still. It's like watching someone sleeping. You suddenly see who they are behind the wall. It gives you time to understand, because you can come out from inside your own defences and just enjoy them.*

*Greg has slipped into his own little world with a slight smile as he writes. I look at Martin's empty desk and think of the way he covers his whole book with his arm, just in case anyone has telescopic vision, and might see what he is putting on the page.*

*Travis is holding his pen like he knows it is a scorpion or something which could fight back. He writes slowly, which is so annoying for someone who thinks and talks so fast. It won't be long before he is so pissed off furniture starts to move. There'll be warning signs first though, and Billy is keeping an eye out for them as well. Not that they're easy to ignore, because Travis starts to shift around a lot first. Like a grizzly bear in a highchair.*

*I go over and offer him some help. He's writing about Jago and the words come flooding out ...*

**Travis** *on Jago*

*"ive chosen jago coz hes nt a mane caractr bt hes importnt. Hes mutch yunger thn the otha lads an skwl is jst startin to go rong for him. When hes introduced it says that he s a difrent story altogether bt he kind of fits th mold. We ar sposed to see jago like a bit of a mascot for the older boys bt ther is more to it thn that. Jago needs sm back up an he dosnt find it anywere els. skwl sees us (the boys) as the worst peopl in the skwl that no 1 shud want to hang out with. We ar nothin bt truble. jagos in btween too lives at skwl. we ar helpin him to keep goin. Its too simple to see us as a bad influens. We look out for jago. he is like the seekwal to th story. or the preekwal maybe."*

\* \* \*

### Greg *on Greg*

"Im writin about Greg coz he is the most charismatic character in the story. All the girls want him badly which is hardly surprising. He is influential ((good word ey??)) and makes a lot of decisions about what is goin on. He is always savin situations like when he goes back to set up the weblink when they break into school. He's not afraid of anything n he thinks christie is a dick sometimes. it ws cool wen he nicked those keys out of the door and locked the caretaker in bt I think miss wrote it like that to big him up a bit coz we give him shit. its true tho about Christie being cheerful and always excited when things get funny. Thats a good trait coz it gets things going especially when school is borin. Greg is a strong character and he cant be doin with bullshit. Who can blame him for that!"

\* \* \*

### Billy *on Miss Rusty*

"Miss Rusty is the narrator of the story. She tells about how she sees us \*The Boyz\* and what she thinks we get up to. She also tells how she feels from the other side as a teacher of a tough class. You can tell that she fancies me loads of course!!! HA! She shows us as her favorites even though we get up to some crazy stuff. she should put in a good sex scene before the end. That would get us into reading for sure! Get the hint Misseeee?*?*?*?*"

\* \* \*

I think about Martin on Death Row. I wonder what he's doing ... I'm getting used to writing about him, to say things which can't just be said.

*He'll be sitting very low in his chair with one elbow on the exam desk put out for him to work on. His hand is resting his head maybe. It must have been a long afternoon. Christie is round a corner at the other end of the corridor. They've probably had some trouble already for making stupid noises loud enough to travel the gap.*

*Martin has his headphones on by now I bet. It makes the world bearable. Like watching TV with the sound turned down- you pretty much know what's going on in front of you, but you don't get sucked in. You can lose yourself totally in tunes. Music can get you through just about anything. It is fucking miraculous what music can do.*

*I'd hazard a guess that he's listening to something which armours him with the hypocrisy of it all. It won't take long before someone comes along and notices he's hooked up to his phone. If that someone pushes for confiscation, Martin will be outta there in a second. There'll be a whole heap of trouble, but he's not going to let anyone near his phone is he?*

*Thinking about Martin got me on to the idea that it was high time I had myself assessed as well. So I put the first five chapters in an envelope and gave them to my Headteacher to see what he thought. We were short on strategies for dealing with the boys as you can probably imagine, and although the book was going well, it wasn't exactly conventional. I was delighted when it was praised. I was delighted, and so were the boys, who again saw a side to authority they hadn't expected at all, and I treasured the envelope upon which my boss had written such warm words of encouragement.*

*That lesson where we did the assessment was the last time I saw Billy. He disappeared completely. No-one, official or unofficial, gave an answer for that one. He left his uniform with me as usual, so he could go straight out from school for his Friday evening. Seemed like he'd just 'done one,' which could mean anything.*

*I miss his challenging personality, and the way he made me feel like he let me win sometimes, as a means of encouragement.*

"Leonora, thanks for letting me read this (an R.S Mock Exam invigilation provided the rest of the time I needed). Initially I wasn't sure about how it would work as a concept but I think it is a triumph. After the first chapter I began to feel really engaged and was fascinated by the idea of the school break in. How I wish we really did have a CCTV tape of 'Greatest Hits'; we wouldn't have come up with such a funny idea! I'd like to come along and talk to the lads about this (in a positive way of course) to have a conversation and to pass on my congratulations – a very different conversation from those I've often had with them previously. You've done a superb job with this. Let me know if I can help."

The Envelope
April 2008

# Stop! Don't read this!
## Chapter 6

So, where were we? In a many legged heap at the bottom of a long, steep staircase which had vanished with the light, leaving nothing but bruises to show it had ever been there.

It seemed insane that just by standing up, the boys had moved far enough away from the bottom of the steps to have no reference point at all in the blackness. I can imagine the way they got to their feet though; separately, in the same space, making a drama out of it, moving more than necessary, being unhelpful.

Down in the dark, Travis stood on Christie's hand and didn't seem to notice until being shoved by Christie's other hand made him fall over Greg who was still feeling round for his mobile. Martin was trying to find the steps in that way he has of being everywhere at once which wasn't much help at that moment, and added to that, there was the smell of Billy's trainers which was somehow much stronger there in the warm darkness. The steps were nowhere close.

"What the fuck is this place?" Greg spoke quietly but the sound seemed to travel.

"I bet it's the old corned-beef store," said Travis, showing his secret interest in history. "The school was used as an army storage facility in the second world war before it ever was a school." Thanks for the history lesson Travis. "There could be dead Nazis down here!" More interesting, but unlikely.

"I bet this is where that kid Daniel Beaver was hiding!" suggested Christie.

"He wasn't real you idiot!" Travis pointed out. Christie knows this perfectly well, but there's never much point explaining it when someone takes a joke literally. Let it go.

The darkness carried on being just as dark as before. You could hold your hand up in front of your face and not see it at all. It's really frustrating not being able to see. Something had to be done, and fast. There was a largeness about the darkness, that made it feel like it was pressing in, while it went on for miles. It was going to get hard to take pretty soon.

They spread out, keeping up the chat so they wouldn't lose each other, trying to find the steps. Christie and Greg tried out a few of their 'Orgasmic Moan Specials', but somehow that entertainment didn't work too well in the pitch dark. It sounded so much like the soundtrack to some teenage gay porn that they gave it up pretty quickly.

As they moved apart, each became focused on their own experience, and the talking dried up. Your senses get sharper in such moments, but when your hearing is working at full speed and you don't hear anything, and your eyes are looking like crrrazy and you don't see anything, it messes with your head a bit. Like when you've got yourself into a whole lot of trouble and you turn the same problem over and over, and every way out of it is blocked by an angry parent, or a pissed off friend, or a finished girlfriend. Sucks!

Christie had found a wall and was feeling his way along it. It was reassuring to come into contact with something familiar, but the plaster was crumbly and there were trickles of something sticky and bitter-smelling here and there which he didn't enjoy putting his hand on.

Travis moved forward purposefully, one hand out in front of him waiting to touch something, and sliding his feet to avoid suddenly walking over the edge of something. Alert as he was, it took him by surprise when he found a smooth round object, firmly fixed, at about waist height. (That's chest height if you're not Travis btw). He felt it for a second or two, before realising it was a door knob, and putting out his other hand to find the door. He'd already turned it, and pushed the door open, by the time his head caught up with what was happening, and he started to feel uneasy.

Sometimes a door opens on a room you are supposed to be entering and it just feels like the room doesn't want you there. Travis had that feeling now.

Whatever was behind the door was hostile, and he didn't really want to go in. His senses were working overtime, focused on the darkness through the doorway of the room he couldn't see. It felt more concentrated in there. Like there was something else in the darkness, facing him, waiting for him to move closer. He could hear his own heartbeat loudly all of a sudden. He froze.

Greg was advancing at low level, still hoping to come across his mobile. The floor was not really the place for one of his fabulous jumpers. It was uneven and gritty, littered with rubbish and broken chairs, and other debris hard to identify.

He turned round and worked his way back, thinking that there hadn't been this much stuff around when they landed, and thinking of plans which were being interrupted by this unexpected situation. It's funny what comes into your head when you are suddenly right outside your comfort zone. You really start to realise what actually matters and what is just entertainment.

In fact, I'm not going to even try and imagine what Greg was thinking, but I guess he wasn't entirely concentrating on what he was doing. Thinking either works as a tranquilliser or an energiser for Greg, but either way he's always at it. He was just about to call out to the others to get the direction right, when he brushed against something that cut through his thoughts completely. He stopped dead, and even though he really didn't want to, he put out his hand again to confirm what he'd just touched. There was a slight shifting rattle as he jumped back.

Maybe it's somewhere deep in our instincts that we can recognise human remains even from one quick touch in the dark. Greg calmed himself by thinking about that one, while he felt his way over a dry arm and across part of a ribcage. The bones shifted again under his jumpy hand. He didn't want to go as far as the skull.

Greg stayed very still, feeling as if the darkness was watching for his reaction, not wanting to shout into it. He didn't move his hand away this time. Somehow he felt he would keep calmer if he knew exactly where the bones were. The moment wound a bit tighter and then several things happened at once.

There was a muffled crash, followed by an unmuffled yell that cut through the darkness, and a sudden glare of light burned into their eyes. The scene looked like an extreme staging of a Year Nine drama production when the lights suddenly go up. There was Christie, poised with his hand on the light switch he'd just come across set into the wall. He was looking just as surprised by the light as if someone else had switched it on. Martin was trying to find a way to climb back up from a kind of well in the floor he'd just fallen into (which explains the crash and the yelp anyway), still moving as if he hadn't realised that the light was now on. Travis was standing as if turned to stone, gazing in horror through the doorway of a broom cupboard. Like he was waiting to be executed by the couple of old sweeping brushes inside it. Greg was staring in complete disbelief at an old Biology classroom skeleton, which lay in disrepair amidst the other school junk scattered around. He almost looked disappointed, as if he'd faced up to the fear of the dead for nothing. They were far closer together than they had thought they were, in a lofty old storeroom with doors leading off it.

They looked at each other, not quite smiling yet, but getting pretty close. Then a loud rumbling roar began which seemed to surround the old walls, causing plaster dust to trickle down from the cracks and before they could get their wits together, the lights went out again, and the darkness came back blacker than before.

*You must unlearn what you have learned.*

*Yoda*
The Empire Strikes Back

*When studying to become a teacher, we are told emphatically and with absolute conviction that we should under no circumstances try to be friends with our students. I don't really get it. By definition a friend is a person who you know, like and trust. It doesn't mean you have to wear matching outfits, tell each other all your secrets and expect a sulk if you queue up for dinner with someone else. Who wants those kind of friendships anyway? I think the whole teacher/student relationship thing goes a bit wrong right from that point. All my life I've had vertical friendships – which is to say that age and social standing are irrelevant in the way I find friends. I choose those whose souls seem to be of a similar age to mine, rather than their bodies or their minds. I've met some ancient people with souls still wrapped in cellophane, like a first edition collector's model of The Millenium Falcon, unplayed with for forty years, and I've known twelve year-olds wiser than great grandparents. I'm sure this has helped me to relate to my students, but whether they are young souls or old, there's something to know, like and trust about every single one of them.*

*You can't actually be a teacher for more than a couple of lessons without encountering some kid whose life experiences are more advanced (and often more horrific) than your own. Many teachers go through school, sixth form, uni, teacher training and then back into school by the time they are twenty-two. It doesn't make them older than the kids in all ways.*

*Sometimes you meet a kid with an attitude problem compounded by eyes that look down on your whole experience of life. It's disempowering and infuriating when you feel that by your very status as The Teacher you have the right to be right. I can't be the only teacher who has found myself wondering mid-shout what I am doing and how on earth this is supposed to help improve the relationship, but I may be one of the few who chooses to stop at that point and say, "I'm sorry, I don't know why I'm shouting at you like this, or how on earth it is supposed to improve our relationship." The results are astonishingly rewarding. It helps to step down a bit and admit that you don't know everything. It's so much harder when you feel under threat of losing face, or it is until you realize that that is what we are asking the most challenging kids to do every day of their school lives. If we can't do it, how can they?*

*There's a lot of unity to be gained from finding out you are at opposite ends of the same problem. Those kids who look at you and sense you are out of your depth are the hardest kids to win and the most rewarding if you succeed. They usually only appear in ones and twos and when you have thirty other kids to deal with it's tempting to sacrifice the odd tough one on the altar of exclusion for the greater good of the class. Very, very occasionally, as I found with the Commy Boys, the world provides you with a whole class full. There are lessons for all in such a group. Provided that in between the shouting and the face-offs you somehow find a safe way to acknowledge that they are not the only ones who still have a lot to learn.*

*I wanted the boys to see The Void as a metaphor for the dangers of carrying their behaviour into adult life, but they probably knew more about that than I did. The unknown, unfriendly world just beyond school. When I was sent home to wait for my list of allegations, I was completely in the dark. I didn't actually know what I had done. I still felt like I was part of the school, existing under their conditions, but I didn't recognise this bit of the building. People I had trusted, like my headteacher, suddenly felt like dangerous adversaries and people who I'd smiled at once or twice on parents' evenings gave me light at the end of the tunnel.*

*The kids were amazing. They just wouldn't let me give up hope and they somehow took charge of caring for me in my isolation. They made badges with my picture that said 'STOP! don't read this badge!', they sent me a Mother's Day card with hundreds of messages that made me sink down on the kitchen floor and cry happy tears for hours, they created a Facebook site so I could read their thoughts, wrote articles, held meetings, it was unbelievable. One girl sent me a piece of her birthday cake in a little squashy parcel. Travis, force that he is, defended me on the radio. So much for the apathy of youth.*

*As I've said, the support of the community seemed to make the disciplinary panel more hostile, though it did wonders for my long-term prospects of survival. Friendship within the school community may currently be regarded as dangerous and reprehensible – not so in the public school sector – but there are greater and stronger themes in life than what the latest policy directs, especially when they change so rapidly. I was to be disciplined anyway so it's unlikely that my feelings of friendship towards students and their parents in general made much of a difference to that. What they did make a difference to was my ability to survive this cruel process relatively intact. Thank god for the people who believe in you and won't let you quit, even though there were bad days when I resented their encouragement and wished everyone would just sod off and leave me to give in and fail. Their unbelievable support provided me with the attention of the world outside and sustained my belief in the value of kindness and community over a paycheque. Thank god for those people.*

*Greg sent me a message; a powerful and heated explanation of how I would be interrogated in the disciplinary hearing. He said they would trap me in smaller and smaller circles, and that I had to be prepared to protect my integrity from what would inevitably happen. "Don't let them convince you you are not who you are!"*

*He armoured me actually and he was right. I don't know whether I was more impressed or depressed at what he had learned from a system where I had been a teacher and he had been a kid. He knew a lot more than I did. He taught me to keep sight of myself whatever they said about me. What a star. And what a shame.*

# Stop! Don't read this!
## Chapter 7

So here we are starting another chapter in the dark. It seems a shame, especially when the last one started in darkness and ended the same way.

This time at least it was noisy darkness for a change. There was the rumbling which sounded like the walls and the roof crumbling from the inside, and there was everyone yelling at Christie to switch the light back on, and Christie yelling back that it made fuck all difference because it didn't work.

The rumbling began to die away. Then came a shaft of light from the ceiling as someone opened the trapdoor. It looked a bit like those old movies where the spaceship has landed and the extra-terrestrial beings are about to make contact with 'the hoomans'. Except in reverse. The stairs came briefly into view, as did a silhouetted figure slipping out at the top, before the trapdoor banged shut again. Billy!

Martin had already got to the staircase before the light vanished. Not bad after falling down a hole. But let's not forget, on his zippiest days, there's no-one as zippy as Martin. He can be all round you at once before you even know he's there. The rest are close behind despite various 'interactions' on the way with old school junk, lying dangerously still and ready to ambush them in the blackness.

Soon they were standing back in the cleaners' cupboard at the top of the stairs. Doing what you do in those moments, taking the piss out of each other for being freaked out, to forget how near to being freaked out you were yourself. HA!

"Did you see Christie's face when he turned the light on? He was shitting himself!"

"What about Greg getting it on with that skeleton?"

"Well that's better than that fucking whatever-her-name-is you had last week!"

Travis found the shut-off switch at the top of the stairs that Billy must have used to cut the lights again. Billy! Funny, they'd all caught the smell of his trainers again as they'd got back to the bottom of the staircase, and he was long-gone by then.

The boys emerged cautiously into the corridor but as soon as they were out they got that desolate feeling you get when the building has just emptied. After three already. They'd been down there a good hour! No point staying in school any longer than necessary and getting picked up by the ASDTB (After School Detention Brigade).

Now they knew where the lights were it was tempting to go back and explore, but school is school and when three o' clock comes round it is replaced by the world outside and it's time to see what's cracking. The various complexities and simplicities of getting and finishing alcohol and girls. Checking your front in quiet moments between noisy social situations. It can be exhausting. Always looking for something better to happen, or looking for somewhere to just hang out undisturbed, or looking for one person who could make or break your evening.

Anyway, it didn't take long on Thursday for a time to come around when somewhere to lie low was needed, and the rain was too heavy for a pleasant smoking experience to be had.

They were sitting in the diner as usual period one, waiting for the ever bustling figure of Miss Earl to come tripping along, wearing lots of red and with a voice like candy floss. She's got amazing legs, and she wears the kind of heels that tell you she doesn't mind you thinking she's got amazing legs. Although why anyone should have to mind you thinking she's got amazing legs just because she's a teacher is a mystery really. She's just got amazing legs! Maybe they don't work that well as actual legs for getting around on though, coz she's always late.

Greg had one of those cheeky grins he seems to wear quite a lot at the moment. He looks so gorgeous when he has a cheeky grin. Let's just say that by year eleven, he'd had The Cheeky Grin That Broke A Thousand Hearts going on for a while.

Things were moving pretty well for Greg on several fronts, with the added bonus of getting a bit of a break from the system. The hounds have been called off for a while, and a New Tactic is being tried. Detentions are to be given sparingly to Greg Bratley, to help him realise that school is there to help him. Hopefully this initiative might last for just a bit longer than it needs for Greg to start acting like he appreciates it, and take it up a couple of notches for the Bratley Pride and all that.*

Travis was sitting apart from the others, in one of his corridor-shrinking sulks for some reason, where he looks like if all this were a cartoon, he would have one of those little thunderclouds above his head, and the other kids just fall out of the way as he passes through. Not his best look shall we say. It could have been something to do with The Cute Girl. They don't spend much time together any more, not that that kind of thing usually seems to bother Travis much. More to the point, he has just had his nipples pierced, and I should imagine that might make anyone grumpy, especially in the cold weather.

Martin was back to his level self after being in his Remote Mood the past few days. The Remote Mood is one of those where it feels like he knocks back anything you say to him, unless you are far enough away. Martin is a bit weather related. I don't necessarily mean that he is stormy when it's stormy, more like when the weather is bad outside he behaves like he's caged maybe, and when it's sunny outside, you can pretty much guarantee that there'll be something sunny about Martin, even if it's on the inside.

---

* In the original version of the story, it was here that the headteacher was mentioned by name. He came up with the initiative to help Greg so I put it in the story to encourage Greg to appreciate it. This was regarded as a breach of professional standards, confidentiality, data protection etc. Thus the line "Mr X, remarkably decent for a headteacher." has now been removed.

It's all part of that sense you get that Martin is fine so long as he can see the way out.

Christie has been doing a lot of stealth growing. He's really coming out of himself and showing who he is, like people do when they get taller all of a sudden. Pretty tense times for Christie with shit on all sides, and he can still raise a smile out of nowhere. He gets really into a story. He's getting into one now in the diner, that Jago is telling about his dad's school days.

Jago had appeared as Jago does, trundling in looking like Winnie the Pooh: small, in his red junior shirt and his quiet, friendly way. Mitch is there as well, slid down in his seat, listening with that slightly raised eyebrow cynical face that he does, like he's timing Jago while he's the centre of attention.

Mrs Barker walked into the diner from the main staircase end, and probably half wished she'd taken the upper corridor instead when she saw the unofficial looking group of boys sitting by the windows who would have to be tackled.

As she drew nearer, unsure whether the vague animal noises she was beginning to hear were real or imaginary, she spotted Greg and got into a fairly heated discussion with him about his name. For some reason, she thought it was Jack, and didn't want to be corrected. There's no real need to record the details of when and why Greg assumed that name one day for the sake of convenience, but it seemed to have stuck with several teachers.

Things started to get ugly when the surrounding woofs reached a volume which she could no longer pretend might be imaginary and everyone was in for some trouble, so it was MDT (Mass Departure Time). Jago went towards the Science Department, the rest headed for the library corridor, and in seconds Mrs Barker found that the only person left within hearing distance of her shouting, was herself. So she stopped. Then Greg stuck his head back round the door for one last 'woof' which didn't go down too well. Looks like another detention for poor old Jack who must be getting pretty baffled by now at how much his name is linked to trouble when he's such an easygoing chap. The letters must be dropping on his parents' doormat like confetti at the moment, while the Bratley doormat is free from trouble. Happy days.

After that start to the day, the trapdoor seemed like an obvious choice. As the boys looked down from the top of the stairs at the cavernous room full of broken furniture, ancient looking machinery and shadowy doorways, they thought back to how it felt in the dark.

They could see now that they'd fallen quite a long way down the stairs. Like if they'd fallen in the light and been able to see how far they had to go, they might have been quite badly injured.

They picked their way through the main room, amazed that they hadn't smacked themselves on the clutter of overhanging pipe work or the rusted metal piled around. It had seemed emptier when they couldn't see. Odd. It's usually the other way round in the dark – one small thing in a vast expanse of nothing and you can guarantee you're gonna stub your toe on it.

They tried all the doors that led off. Most were filthy store cupboards with shelves full of dusty old crap. One had a scattering of ancient porn mags. There was a pause there for entertainment, and 'ya mum' comments.

Only one door was locked. Travis was making a fair attempt at shouldering it but with no success, till the key fell to the ground with a faint tinkling sound. Some sensible person must have realised long ago that you didn't want to get as far as this door and find you'd forgotten the key, so it lived tucked away on top of the door frame. Christie picked it up and fitted it into the lock. It turned like a lock that has almost forgotten how to turn. With the same stiffness as an old dog getting to its feet after a long sleep.

They are discussing Mrs Barker and The Whole School Thing. Travis is telling Jago how they got onto a school computer which was logged on to the system. They accessed their punishment records to see who had the most detentions and exclusions.

Martin and Billy were the top scorers out of some pretty top scores. Christie kept a look-out by the classroom door. Then Travis looked at Jago's record, just for the hell of it, and discovered that 'little Jago' had more file than any of them! No-one could believe it, except that when they thought about it, it kind of made sense. The kind of sense you don't want life to make.

I mean, why do teachers sometimes just look at the outside of kids, when they know how much they've got inside themselves?

Simple law of the universe – The bigger the front, the bigger the back.

Jago's front has been a bit brittle recently.

They see Maddy sitting on the wall looking tired and glamorous in equal parts. She smiles as they approach and asks Travis if he has seen Greg. He hasn't. Maddy looks like she hasn't seen Greg for a while either. Her eyes drop for a second, and then she recovers it and says hi to Jago. Jago and Travis carry on walking. Travis is into the subject.

"Yeah, we were having a bit of a bet on who had the most punishments, and it was you! We tried all ours, and Martin an' Billy had pages of them, which wasn't very surprising, and we checked a few other people who get in shit quite a bit, but they were nowhere near Martin an' Billy! Greg had loads before, but he's been getting away with tons of shit recently. Mine is bad like you'd expect, but people don't seem to push it that far with me these days coz they're worried about how I'm gonna react probably. Then I tried yours and you've got way more than any of us! Its fucking insane!!"

"I know I've had LOADS recently! I just don't get it at all. When you're having a shit time, it's like you get in so much shit."

Jago hardly comes up to Travis' chest. He speaks softly, and he has honey-coloured skin. You can already tell he's going to be serious eye candy when he's older.

Travis is pissed off about it all. He can sense the way its going for Jago. Travis got labelled years ago when he was having a shit time. He kicked back. He has a lot to say on the subject and it reminds you that really he should be on the school's debating team, not the school's detention list …

"I mean, What is it with schools? It's like, when you're being just how they want you to be it's great and all friendly. But then you just know you're getting yourself tied into behaving like their shallow fucking image of who you really are! It does my head in!! Step one way or the other across that line for whatever reason and suddenly you're a fuck-up! It doesn't seem to matter what the reasons are. You could be going through all kinds of shit! If you're one of those drippy girls who just cry all the time, you get away with it, but if you're angry – they just don't know how to handle it. As soon as you start questioning anything, or getting stressed about anything, the shit starts, and just when you most need them to give you a bit of a break, they don't! I swear it's like you have to pretend to be half of what you are so they can go on thinking they're superior, or some shit!! In fact, you know what? Sometimes, school is like a bad dad!!"

A group of kids are walking with them by this point. One of Travis' rants always gathers a crowd. He usually seems to like talking to ten different people at once, but this time, he glances round at the company, and then swings Jago easily up onto his shoulders, like he is a much smaller boy. The group takes the hint and kind of disappears, and Travis continues his speech in a quieter voice. This one is between him and Jago.

"They get scared I swear, when you show your spirit and you need them to expand their ideas. Fuck. They're such fucking hypocrites sometimes. And why don't they realize that if you've got ten detentions for the same thing, it's not really working! How many detentions have you had for swearing? I've had so many detentions for fucking swearing, its hectic! As if they don't swear! And they're so busy trying to make us respect them! There should be more of a reason to respect people than just to save them from feeling like they're out of their depth. They like to pretend *I'm* stupid coz I can't spell properly but they don't really do anything about it!"

Jago is listening carefully to Travis, but he takes his chance to get a word in.

"Yeah, but they're not all like that … " He's thinking about Mr Blero and his oasis of peace. Like being in a greenhouse and just feeling things growing. And Mr Carson, who gets so stressed you think he's going to ignite, and then he suddenly turns it into a joke and gets it back to the science of fast and slow reacting metals or something, and everyone is wide awake.

"Yeah. But plenty of them are!" Travis is off again in 'burning car mode'. Its a long time since he was part of a calm and happy class. The petrol tank could go up at any moment. "I know what you mean, and you're right, some teachers are legends! But that still fits with my 'bad dad' theory. The great parts make the shit parts harder to deal with. It wouldn't get to us if we couldn't see how good school could be. I mean, look at you and all those detentions, you're just an easy target."

"Maybe they think coz I'm younger I can be saved or something … "

"Yeah, but do you feel saved?? Like I said, when everything is going okay, you can't make any sudden movements or the whole fucking spell is broken. And that's shit frankly! I'm telling you, school is like a bad dad!!"

"Yeah, maybe you're right," says Jago, "coz in a weird way, even when it's going shit, you still want it to get who you are, and you still want everything to be okay … "

If he wasn't on Travis' shoulders it would have been too quiet to hear, the way he said it.

I kind of know what Travis is on about, even though he talks like what he is – a young man, with fire in his belly. The problem for the adults is that we grow up to forget that revolution is possible. That you can change the whole course of your life. That you can do courageously stupid things, just because courage is important. And risk is important. And spirit. It's why mothers want you to be happy, but still think you should put your coat on. It's why they want you to have fun, but they won't let you play on the edge of the cliff. It's all down to the children we were, and the children you aren't any more. Does that make any sense at all?

Michael Jackson didn't really invent the Moonwalk. Kids did. Sometimes you see them walking to school like they never plan to arrive, and they still do.

Jago and Travis are doing the Moonwalk now. They've got half a mile to go in the next four minutes and somehow, just by not really wanting to, they'll get there.

It's an argument for believing in Destiny.

***

*Kids talk about punishments incessantly at school: what they got punished for and how unfair it was, or what they did and got away with. The staff talk endlessly about them too. It's hard not to resort to punishments as a quick fix for control in a busy day, and yet it's such a shame when teachers tell kids off like they mean to win. As if winning should have any part of showing someone how to behave. Isn't it meant to be the taking part?*

*We want our young people to learn to do the right thing because it's the right thing, not because you could get into trouble if you don't. Everyone has a deep-seated longing to do well and be acknowledged for it. Everyone. As soon as a teacher really understands that about kids, it becomes clear that those who aren't doing well have something in the way, and that inflicting punishment is a form of retribution which only makes their problems worse.*

*When I stopped using the punishment system, my need for it disappeared. Such a system is useful when you first start teaching – you've got to have some sort of arsenal when you are a rookie, or the kids would have you for breakfast and the classroom would be just plain dangerous. There's too much to learn about classroom dynamics to go all hippied out about detentions, but once you have a grip of all that, you have the space to build a reputation and a chance to be more creative. You don't carry on using stabilisers once you can ride a bike.*

*Patrick was Trav's mate. They'd known each other since they were three years old. One blond, one dark; one broad, one skinny; one at ease with school, one far from it. It's funny how from the back or the front, they still looked like brothers. At the age of eighteen, some time after they'd left school, Patrick was killed in a car crash half-way across the world. He was having a great time, and he deserved to have a great time just about as much as a person can deserve a great time.*

*I spent the day with Trav just after it happened. We walked the dogs in the woods, drank tea and ate ginger biscuits sitting on the kitchen counter. We spoke to the press and agreed to find them a photo of Patrick – well we didn't want them trawling up some goofy primary school picture and plastering that everywhere. Although to tell you the truth it would be just about impossible to find a cuter primary school kid than Patrick was. We looked through Trav's phone, and there was Patrick on the tree swing just before he left for The States. He was wearing a red tee shirt, brightly focused, mid swing in a haze of blurred green. He looked serenely happy, swinging on the moment.*

*Between biscuits we talked about the unfairness of it all. Patrick was universally clean-living and kind. If Travis had been killed, getting up to wild things as he did, it wouldn't have surprised anyone. Trav said it was Patrick out of all his mates that should have been around to bury him. Patrick never even drank. He wrote bloody good poems and thought-provoking articles, got involved in the community, and facilitated all the social lives of our local parents with his endless babysitting.*

*I can't help seeing Patrick as an example of what goes wrong with punishing kids. It runs contrary to the planet, it is spinning the wrong way. In life terrible things happen. Random, terrible things happen all the time to people who don't deserve them, and we see plenty of cruel people flourish. We can't stop such injustice, but why should we risk adding to it? However hard you try, punishment in school is never truly fair or consistent, because the world simply isn't fair: not everyone gets caught, not everyone has had the same start to the day, not everyone has support, and not everyone has actually done what they are supposed to have done. Children who get into a lot of trouble know this and start to see punishment as an arbitrary trick of fate for which they somehow got singled out and which somehow attracts more and more punishment. Once they see it in this way, the chances of repeated sanctions actually modifying their behaviour slip down below zero, becoming detached from whatever the child is supposed to have done. You can't exactly respect a punishment if you don't think it's fair, so it's hardly likely to make you respect the person who gave it to you.*

*I cannot pretend to ignore the fact that kids who haven't had any breakfast often get in more trouble than those who have. So do those who've lost a parent, or are unusually tall for their age. So do those who are the only fat kid, or the only black kid, the one who can't spell, or the only one with bright ginger hair. And when the detentions mount up we say they are their own worst enemy. Because life isn't actually fair.*

*I know I ramble on a lot about teachery things, but it's pretty simple stuff really that can be applied to more than a classroom. I talked to an ex-student, Will, a while back when he came home from college for Christmas. It's lovely when they pop round for a cup of tea and tell you how life is going out there.*

*Like folks do, he'd met his new best friend in the registration queue on the very first day. They were both there to study music, and the embryo new best friend, a cheerful stocky lad with curly hair and a singsong Welsh accent, asked Will which composers he was into. Will explained that he was keen to impress the embryo new best friend, so he flashed out some name of some avant garde composer who created cacophonies for people in pashminas at London soirees to show off about, before asking the embryo best friend the same question in return. The embryo best friend smiled affably and said, "Well, I don't think you can beat a bit of Mozart myself", the undeniable honest simplicity of which out-cooled old Will and his modern ponce completely.*

*The embryo new best friend then became the real best friend, and as best friends do, they laughed heartily over that first chat later. It's the kind of moment that makes a great assembly. We all get so enmired in pseudo-sophistication and psycho-babble that we lose sight of the most obvious things. The embryo new best friend was right, you can't actually beat a bit of Mozart, and what Mozart is to music, friendship and kindness is to kids. Kindness. Creative kindness if you can muster it when it's needed most, but it's knackering writing novels on a Thursday evening so thank god plain old friendly kindness is generally all it takes. It doesn't matter how hard a kid you are, you can't fight back against kindness and think you are winning for long.*

*Whether you are winning or not.*

*An article written by Trav's mate Patrick when I was suspended and he was just 16 years old ...*

OH, hurrah for our teaching standards! Thank goodness we choose to rigorously asses our public officials, should they show a whiff of forbidden initiative!

Thank goodness we stopped that awful Rustamova woman before she did the unspeakable and genuinely connected with her students!

This, I can only assume is the skewed logic that must have flitted through the head of whoever triggered the 'petty complaint' alarm, which has been popular of late.

I am talking, of course about the suspension of local teacher Leonora Rustamova: teacher being rather an understatement if students' reactions, and accounts I have heard from students in her group are anything to go by.

For those unfamiliar with the workings of secondary schools, 'difficult' children in the year tend to be collated into one group. Although the mere idea of teaching the group causes most teachers to go weak at the knees, Rustamova was amongst an elite few who not only took on the job, but relished it, gaining that rare thing for a teacher amongst troubled students, respect and even friendship.

I'd never seen my dyslexic friend so enthusiastic about going to a lesson, and have definitely never seen students rebel en masse over possible suspension of a teacher.

As for the book itself, I am among the lucky few to have read it. I can assure readers that the nearest thing any child-proud parent could so much as frown at is its portrayal of the students in question as charismatic heroes.

Alas though, for some reason as yet unexplained to us, the book has come dangerously close to dampening the cotton wool any state institution finds it necessary to smother children in. And any information that might lead us to realise what pathetic, bureaucratic, and misdirected 'justice' is going on has been withheld!

However, to the point of my letter: please let us not forget the effect her removal might have, disillusioning those students who looked to her as security in the school environment they found so difficult.

And let's not allow a book symbolising exactly how exceptional teachers can reform and support even the most difficult students become the reason for a dedicated, passionate individual to lose their job.

Patrick Munsie
*Hebden Bridge Times*
Thursday 12th February 2009

*Patrick was ace.*

# Stop! Don't read this!
## Chapter 8

Their final year was moving on. Time does weird things when you are near the end of something. Each individual school minute drags by, while the actual whole weeks go really fast.

I'm not sure how many days or weeks the boys were using the underground void as a useful hangout, or even when they first found it; the weather was still cold, and the corridors had someone to hassle kids on every intersection, so The Void became the regular chance for a getaway.

After they discovered the guard's room behind that last locked door, or 'HQ' as it came to be known, they must have settled in quite quickly. I only went down there one fateful day and it looked pretty set up to me, with a presumably 'borrowed' school laptop on the table, all the most comfortable or least broken chairs which had been collected up from around the place were grouped round the table and the shelves were piled up with random stuff.

The vintage porn had found its way in there of course, as had the Biology skeleton which sat in a chair with a school shirt on and with evidence to suggest that it was used regularly for target practice. There were beer bottles and even ashtrays – pretty sorted as I said, but it's not every day you find such a useful place in a school so it had to be treated with some respect at least.

I remember wondering who would have been the most likely of the boys to have come up with the idea of treating the place with a bit of respect, and I found it could really have been any of them, which made me smile.

They'd had time to settle in anyway, and time to search around for the white boxes which had led them to the Void in the first place. They'd been quite keen, and even adopted Travis's suggestion that they should search systematically after the first sweep revealed nothing, they got distracted for a while by other things which they found on the way. Nothing as exciting as hand grenades but there was quite a bit of old wartime junk, like boxes of candles which were useful if they were down there when the bell went. The lights often conked out when the rumble of the kids moving from one lesson to another began. It was only the 'three o'clocker' that made the walls shake though and the boys were usually out of there by then.

They conducted a couple of other searches but the white boxes went undiscovered and the whole thing got a bit boring and faded out in favour of the more immediate entertainment of the hang out. It was a peachy place to have in school.

There was quite a bit of argument over who should know about it; there were various obvious choices like Jago, and Pudge and current girls who were put forward. But, being the kind of place that would quickly be ruined if too many people got to hear about it, no-one really wanted to turn it into general knowledge. Not till they'd found the boxes anyway. Greg was reluctant to agree to this at first, (especially as there was a narrow bed in the back corner of the guard's room, which must have been there since the days of the army night watch), but he admitted in the end that they should keep the Void quiet, at least for a while, till it got boring. The laptop had been set to screensave with a live shot from the camera up outside the cleaners' cupboard entrance, to warn of any potential visitors.

Then there was the mystery of Billy. It's a real trait in Billy to lie low for a while if he thinks there's something worth avoiding, but no-one had seen or heard of Billy since he shut off the lights and did one out of the trapdoor. It was hardly worth avoiding school for that. Things that bother you in the dark often disappear as soon as the lights come back on, and Billy had done far worse things in his time without feeling the need to make any kind of a getaway. So where was Billy? As time went by it began to seem stranger and stranger. Why had he run off like that anyway? He had been as curious as anybody about what might be down there. No-one mentioned that they still got a faint reminder of the smell of those trainers when they passed the bottom of the stairs, but they had all had it. Smells are supposed to be more of an aid to memory even than music (which I doubt) and it seemed almost like a memorial to Billy the way they all silently relived that smell when they passed that spot. So where the fuck was Billy?

The answers to both questions, Billy and the Boxes (sounds like the name of a late seventies punk band), were somewhat intertwined as it turned out, and they both broke on the scene at the same time and had the kind of impact you would experience if you happened to be around on a hilltop in Geneva when Dr Frankenstein was just harnessing the lightning to zap his monster to life and you got caught in the crossfire.

Anyway, the hangout had been in use for a fair old while by this time. Christie liked to go down there occasionally just to be on another plane to the pressures at street level. He was often there before the others. Martin was in one of his 'caged animal' trekking phases and was usually first to leave. He liked the Void for a bit of a break but he is a true product of the hilltops and didn't like the SBV (Subterranean Bunker Vibe) too much.

There was a bit of competition going on over jumping off the staircase. Every day the record for the best jump down went up by a couple of steps. It was getting close to the height that they had originally fallen from. Then Martin took it into his head to jump on the unsuspecting Travis who was walking past beneath. He had been half way up the stairs, about to embark on a wander, when he'd seen Travis foraging around and without thinking, he launched himself off a step not too very far from the top. Martin has done some scary leaps in his time, off bridges and all sorts of things, but this one was a real bad-boy of a jump. He hit Travis hard and they both continued to the floor which let out a hollow, echoey, thud as they hit it, as if you could almost hear it defining the corners of something clanky like a ship underneath. Weird. Travis forgot to even call Martin a dick for landing on him so unexpectedly.

Closer inspection revealed that the floor in this area was made up of loose boards which stretched back into the gloom under the stairs. In the darker recess, some of the boards were missing and the boys wondered, as one does in such moments, why they hadn't noticed before. Maybe because there was none of the usual junk under there so it hadn't seemed worth investigating.

They leaned over the hole in the floorboards but it was way too dark to see anything. Martin went off to get candles from the guard's room. Travis sat down with his legs stretched out of the shadow and his back against the staircase. He shut his eyes and rested his head back.

When Martin reappeared with Greg and Christie and the candle, Travis was almost asleep. He woke up pretty quickly when a lighted candle was held to his arm though.

"Dickhead!"

Greg got the candle and held it over the broken boards and they all peered in. They couldn't see far, but they all saw the dim, ghostly white outline of boxes down below. There were three of them visible, just beyond arm's reach. Christie lay down on his side and tried to reach in as far as possible. There was a slick, oily smell coming up from the hole, with a hint of decay.

"Smells like rats man!" he was just starting to say when his fingertips brushed against something which moved. Christie jumped up trying not to look freaked and Travis took up the challenge. He sat on the edge of the hole and let himself down into the darkness, keeping an eye on

Greg and the candle. Supporting his weight on his arms, he felt around gingerly for a foothold.

There's water down here!" he reported, "an it stinks". His feet found firm ground towards the left hand side and he was soon standing with his back against a wall he couldn't see, on a kind of shelf next to the pool. Greg passed him the candle. There was a kind of underfloor storage tank which filled most of the space. It had rusted sides and was partially covered with a rotten wooden lid. The white boxes were piled on top of the lid, fairly smeared with grime, but there was little doubt that these were in fact the boxes they were looking for.

"Get a lid off one of em!" said Greg, his voice sounding strangely distant as it came down through the hole.

Travis found a pipe sticking out of the wall which seemed solid, and held on to it so that he could lean far enough over the tank to reach the nearest box. It was made of some kind of strong polymer, a hard light plastic, easy to carry, and protective of the contents. Travis looked up to get some help with holding the candle and laughed at the little circle of faces stuck round the top of the hole. They looked younger somehow in the candle light. Like little kids up after bedtime and peering down the stairs to get a look at the party.

Martin reached down and took the candle, holding it steady over the tank. Travis stretched towards the box with his now spare hand. The lid snapped off smartly as it was designed to do, and the boys had one of those 'still believe in Father Christmas' flashback feelings, you know like you get if someone truly manages to surprise you with a gift that you always always wanted. There was a kind of general gasp from everyone, and then they all started laughing and shouting at once. The laughter had an ethereal effect, with the usual airy echo from the Void, and a deep lonely echo from the hole under the floor.

The box was packed immaculately neatly with small plastic bags of an all too familiar and all too expensive white powder. Holy fuck. Cocaine? It had to be. Holy fuck!

The boys wasted no time organising Travis into handing up the box, and leaning back over the tank to slide the next one into a position where he could lift it. He had to be careful as the tank was huge and the lid was rotten through in quite a few places. The smell was one of those which gets worse the longer you are in it, not better. A smell with layers.

Two of the boxes were safely out. They worked quietly now, each one's mind racing around the awesome prospect of what they had found. Thinking it through. Trying to establish it as part of the new reality. Estimating dangers and possibilities.

Travis leaned as far as he could to shove the last box. It was lodged over a gap in the lid so he had to be careful for it not to fall in. On closer inspection, the stinking liquid turned out to be some kind of heating oil: old and evil and long past its sell-by date, you wouldn't want to touch anything that had been in there.

As he shoved the box, dislodging it, part of the lid crumbled away and fell into the tank, and something bobbed into view from beneath the oily surface. Travis froze. His heart went cold and he actually felt the hairs on his arms standing on end. He stared uncomprehendingly at the heels of Billy's trainers, before they slipped silently back under the surface.

# Stop! Don't read this!
## Chapter 9

Stop the world for a minute here. I mean it's all fine and dandy all those movies where the dead drop like skittles, but this is Billy we're talking about. Billy has a cheeky answer for everything and if he hasn't, he can still get away with whatever he's done to you just by laughing, lying low and being Billy about it, but he can't exactly billy his way out of this one. When something like that happens, the traditional principles of thought and feeling go away and leave you without a system.

Somehow Travis must have confirmed for the others what they'd glimpsed from above. Somehow he must have got out of the hole and somehow they must have tried to come to terms with what had happened to Billy.

Seems unimaginable now, that even after some pretty awful nightmares in some pretty awful nights, inter-cut with pretty hazy lazy last days of school life, they managed to leave all thoughts of Billy down there with the oil tank for a good few days after that. Seems unimaginable, but reactions to death are unimaginable, so the images of Billy floating there in oil like a specimen in a science lab were somehow pushed into some containable corner of their minds. You could call it horrifying the way they locked out the Billy Thing. Or you could call it shock. Call it what you like, they didn't even get as far as really wondering about who it was that must have pushed Billy in, before shutting off the lights and escaping through the trapdoor. Too much to cope with, so they just shut it out.

The sun finally and unexpectedly came out in their last term of Year 11. No-one enjoys a sunny day like the British do. Coz a sunny day in England always feels like a blessing. Two in a row and it turned into a mini festival down at the park with 'Skivers United' in their red and blue colours, chillin' away bits of the day, and drifting in and out of school in a half-hearted way.

The white boxes had been re-stashed at the far end of the Void, although little thought had gone into how to deal with that one.

Somehow thinking about it was too closely associated with Billy to be done just yet. Then for no apparent reason, there were suddenly only a few days of school left before exam leave started. It's a hard one to get your head round. You look forward to getting out for so long, and then when it comes to it, you start to feel rather more affectionate about school. At least the teachers are supposed to care while they boss you around, not just boss you around. And school is a rich social network after all. You have to get a bit sentimental when you're leaving.

So, when none of the boys were there for their last ever English lesson, I suppose I felt like things were getting a bit out of hand. I'd been observing the unusual amount of interest they showed the cleaners' cupboard for a while. They were pretty foxy about sneaking in and out unnoticed, but sometimes you're supernaturally aware of your favourites. You know, like you often just know where your mates are, so you go there, and they are. Up till then I'd thought the cleaners' cupboard was none of my business really, but as I say, it was our last ever English lesson, and not a rosy-cheeked, sun-kissed, lightly-stoned, half-pissed face in sight! In the last few weeks it seemed like nearly all of them had invited some 'police interest', but you can't get arrested when you've got English in the afternoon! That's just not right.

I headed for the cleaners' cupboard. Jago, aka Winnie the Pooh, was trundling along beside me loaded up with the tea order, looking more like Winnie the Beetroot after a lively lunchtime out in the sunshine. Before we knew it we were heading down the dusty steps. I hated it. It reminded me of that movie 'Silence of the Lambs'. I felt small, and out of my depth in a strange place, where nothing should be strange.

We didn't get to see the boys though, 'til after a whole load of shit had gone down. For all we knew, the abandoned tray of teas with its accompanying sugar mountain could have stayed down there, fossilised, till the end of time.

But that's all in the last chapters which I can't read aloud. I don't do all that 'The End' stuff if I can possibly avoid it. You'll have to read the rest of it yourselves.

*** 

*It took a while to get this far with the story. I was writing the chapters week by week and I only read them out on Friday if all the boys were present. Due to their distressed school careers there were sadly many occasions when at least one of them had been excluded by Friday, so progress with the story was slow.*

*I finished it into a book in my summer holidays, sitting on a sunbed in Egypt, pulling the loose pages together and scribbling towards the end while my family tolerantly got on with Holiday Things around me. I was still determined that we should get to the end of a book, and still determined to show the boys how much they mattered and to let them know that, even though school was behind them, the journey didn't stop there. Thus chapter nine concludes, You will have to read the rest of it yourselves ... Which to my delight, even though they had left school five months before receiving the completed book, they all did.*

*It would've been insanely expensive to have a printhouse bind enough copies into something that looked like a book, and it had to look like a book. So my husband suggested using a print-on-demand website and kindly volunteered to format it (whatever that means) and send me the finished products. He liked the whole idea of the story and wanted to do this for the kids. Unfortunately I am no I.T. expert myself, in fact as my daughter likes to point out, electronic equipment has a tendency to just stop working if I enter the room, which is how when it came to producing printed copies, it ended up publicly available on the internet.*

*Its readership up to the point of my suspension totalled some teachers from the school, the characters and their parents, a nice boy from my year group, the Head, my mum and dad, my mate Rosie and my Auntie Marjorie (okay I haven't got an Auntie Marjorie). Anyway, at that point it is fair to say 'STOP! Don't*

Read This!' had hardly polluted and endangered a generation. When the printed copies arrived I gave one to my Headteacher for approval, with a note to remind him of the salient details. It's remarkable how many times that note has come to be read and its motives analysed since then. The note begins, 'I thought you ought to have the opportunity of looking this over before we meet in court.' Oh dear. A couple of years later, I sat in a courtroom listening to this note being discussed in legalese, and Rosie sitting beside me festooned in lever arch files, whispered, 'All this legal stuff is not you. I'm bored of all these processes!' Pointing at the page with the note on it she added, 'This is you! I like You! When can we just have You back?'

I thought you ought to at least have the opportunity of looking this over before we meet in court ... It is a lawless work I'm afraid, but the characters just made it that way. There was no winning without showing them I knew who they were. After all we have to know them and love them anyway to have any impact.

So you know ... sorry about the swearing, the outrageous liberties I've taken with the building, and the familiar approach to my students (it's like a microcosm of my career now that I look back at the beginning of this sentence), I felt I had to step into their world to be any use to them at all. And in return they've taught me invaluable things about the furthest outposts of inclusion and gotten me through the year. I wanted them to know that in the name of stories you can say what you wouldn't normally say, and show what you wouldn't normally show. And I wanted them to feel that a book doesn't have to have its force in what actually happens, that you can journey through yourself between the plot. But I suppose most of all I wanted them to have something to remind them that they were more than just a job in the moments when they need reminding because their worst problem lies in feeling unvalued. Couldn't think of any other way of doing it that they'd approve of ...

*Note to the Head accompanying the complete printed copy of the book.*

*September 2008*

*If you invite a pig to dinner it will put its feet on the table.*

Russian proverb

*** 

*The boys had a lot of exclusions, for varying misdemeanours, although I tried to help them navigate the last few months of school as best I could. It was of great importance for them to complete the final year without being permanently excluded if they were to have any hope of going on to college or training placements subsequently. Although they were all still very close to the edge at that time, their change in trajectory was deserving of a smooth transition to the next step in life. We had a calm and supportive relationship well established between us in the good old Ghetto, where we drank tea, did our work, talked about great themes, the universe and what went down at the weekend. I wanted them to be able to take what we had achieved together and expand it out into life, find it in other places, uphold it as a value. I wanted the same for myself if I am honest.*

*They asked me if we could have an event of some sort to celebrate their leaving school. I agreed to this not merely as a celebration but as a major incentive to help them focus on avoiding permanent exclusion. I didn't too much fancy the idea of going out to a pizza joint or anywhere near a bar with them, given the friction that often resulted from their evenings around the general public at that time. They had been paintballing the year before, and loved it, and I had heard the stories of the way they'd reinterpreted the safety instructions to include the pulling off of masks and the shooting of each other point blank in the face. All very entertaining if you happen to be a wild youth, but not really my idea of a good time.*

*Despite the advent of Health and Safety, there is an age old code of the North which makes it essential in certain circumstances to accept pain as hilarious. Such wholesome pursuits as being hunted down mercilessly like a rabbit and suffering physical harm from one's companions, fall firmly into this category, by which I mean that the more harm they do you, the more you have to laugh about it. I had spent the best part of a year building up my tenuous alpha female status in this group, and was anxious not to enter any situation that might knock me right back down to a rabbit. Going all out on the animal imagery as we come into the final furlong of this paragraph, paintballing ran the risk of becoming the socio-educational equivalent for me of rolling a six and landing in the jaws of that last great beast on the snakes and ladders board that slithers you all the way back to square one. We settled on the idea of a barbecue.*

*It was to be held after they had left school and finished their exams, and only those who completed their school life were to be allowed to attend. I enlisted the help and support of my English colleague and very dear friend Steve and arranged for this event to be held at his house. He lives in a rambly old place out in the countryside, but within the school catchment, his daughters both went to our school, his neighbours' kids went there as well so it seemed like an appropriate venue. A couple of older ex-students who knew the boys, offered to come along and help out.*

*We took some pains as regards the issue of alcohol consumption, with a realistic awareness of how teenagers skulk around with bottles of grog in their pockets, swigging it here and there in unmeasurable quantities. Neither myself nor Steve would have been comfortable without some realistic plan to counter such unquantifiable risk. When teenagers – especially boys – drink with other teenagers they often see a good evening as measured by the total units of alcohol survived, which let's face it, is something well worth growing out of. We saw this event as an opportunity to reinforce mature and moderate social drinking as an embellishment to a dinner, so we devised a full scale treasure hunt with clues which ranged over the hillside and involved some hearty digging at the end to raise a box containing a couple of bottles of beer each and some shiny looking sweets. The exhumation coincided with the food arriving on the table. Steve, an enviable cook, provided us with mountains of juicy meat, even stepping down from his usual levels of culinary refinement to make chips as well for Greg who wouldn't eat anything else in those days.*

*We had just finished dinner and were sitting round our bellies, round the table in the back parlour. It is so very Jane Austen of Steve, to have a back parlour with a Steinway grand piano in it, that I had to ask him to play. He is no Mary Bennet however so it took a while to persuade him into it: a troublesome task which reminded me of how I had baulked myself back in the day when faced with reading out that first chapter.*

*He chose Chopin's Revolutionary Study and as the music filled the house, I looked round at the faces of the Commy Boys. They were all listening so attentively, that something welled up inside me which turned into a giggle. I tried to hide it like you do when such a response turns up inappropriately, and it got worse. Then Rosie, a former student of mine who somehow one day imperceptibly became my kid sister, caught the humour of it and made it worse still. The boys were shooting me disgusted looks for being so rude and the role reversal got to me so badly that I was shaking with laughter by the end of the piece and tears were running down my face.*

*It was a moment of relief I suppose, at the journey we had taken together through Year Eleven ending out so sweetly. Such a decent bunch of lads, so loyal and appreciative, so pleasant to hang out with, and so recognisably themselves. They still reproach me for my rudeness in Steve's recital, even though for form's sake, I like to insist it was all their fault.*

*Later in the night we went out into the hayfield and sat on the well top while some smoked and all were quiet. We live in a complex part of the country but we are not city folk. I was thinking, not about anything in particular, more in the way that you can gaze up at the stars, knowing that there are constellations, but not look for them, because you are just gazing at the stars. A nice kind of thinking. It's important sometimes to make sure you have a feel for the whole sky before you try to seek out the connections.*

*I thought that I had worked a change in the Commy Boys until they left school and I remained. Then I began to understand the change they had brought about in me, and only then did I appreciate that none of us had changed. We had merely found ways to bring out different facets in each other through an acknowledgement of ourselves as multi-dimensional. We were not flat ideas to each other any more. The qualities which made my boys so difficult at school were the same ones that made them great company: incisive perceptions, dry humour, leadership, life-experience, courage, streetsmart, the list is long.*

*Educational policy has been messed around so much in recent years that it has become counter-productive, it is alienating our finest human qualities, it is turning positives into negatives and making lions out of foals. When did a troubled child become an enemy of the state? When it needed a helping hand and was given a document instead entitled 'Duty of Care and Safeguarding Regulations' perhaps. It is stated that these rules exist for our own protection as well as the child's. So we can't hug them when they cry any more, because we could be paedophiles or they could pretend we are. We can't be real. Don't touch them and don't love them and everything will be alright. But they are children!*

*All my ranting between chapters about classroom personae and friendship and kindness were ideas that disquieted me increasingly as the rules around education tightened. It is alarming to feel that what you know is right is gradually being outlawed around you. Somehow the Commy Boys turned all that from acres of sky into constellations and once they have been pointed out, you struggle to see the sky without reference to them any more.*

*We discussed chicken dinosaurs in a class one time – not the grey, meat-related novelty shapes in breadcrumbs that some people have for dinner – it was a bit more academic than that. Some kid was telling us about the discovery of frozen dinosaur flesh exposed by the polar ice-cap melt or something. She said that scientists had extracted DNA from it and discovered that the code matched that of birds, but the dinosaury parts had been switched off for the modern world. The scientists went on to find ways of reawakening bits of the code and were producing chickens with beak-teeth and chickens with long scaley tails. It's a staggering idea.*

*We talked about the possibility of visiting a real Jurassic Park in ten years time, an idea I thought would excite them. They sounded keen for a while until one lad pointed out that in the movie, Jurassic Park is horrific. That it is abused and made dangerous by one of its creators trying to steal embryos to sell on the black market, and that the little kids end up being abandoned to fight the carnivores alone. The principles it was set up on don't even hold up as long as the inspection visit, because they fail to take nature into account and give it the respect it deserves.*

*The scientists, brilliant though they are at hatching dinosaurs, and installing cutting edge computerised paddock fences, are unable to predict the behaviours and adaptations of their creations, never mind the hidden agendas of the people in charge. The computer system is only as strong as the man with the password, and despite the precaution of making sure all the adult dinosaurs are female, some develop the ability to reproduce. Nature finds a way, as it were.*

*The discussion grew till a girl said – Yeah what about that bit where that posh bloke leaves them kids with the T-Rex Miss, and saves himself. Some fun park! – which led us on from exploring the motives and responsibility for the experiment and its consequences, into a debate about whether it is socially acceptable to use 'cool' short forms like T-Rex and J-Park or whether that is actually just lame. We concluded it is fairly lame, but works in very small doses, and is a good way of avoiding how to spell Tyrannosaurus (or however you spell it). I love English lessons.*

*In the way of true stories, it was the same boy who'd told us his earliest toyshop memory, that brought up the idea of the adults finding it irresistible to exploit a dinosaur park for their own short term gain. The little blighter really had a remarkable handle on the frailty of authority and its motivations I have to say. Probably because this random reactionary helter skelter of educational policy is somehow making mutant sabre-toothed chickens out of kids just like him. That in the name of caring, it somehow didn't care for lost kids with pride and a position to defend as well as problems.*

*Shouldn't this be stopped before they start breeding in the sewers or whatever it is that mutant sabre-toothed chickens do.*

*"As you know, I don't believe in talking down to children, you are capable of grasping more than is generally appreciated by your elders. Education means leading out, from e, out and duco, I lead. To me education is a leading out of what is already there in the pupil's soul."*

The Prime of Miss Jean Brodie
*Muriel Spark, 1961*

*I hadn't heard from the kid with the toyshop memory for a while, and it's quite a few years now since he left school, or school left him – I don't remember which, then just today he messaged me like some people do the moment you think about them, or put them in your book ...*

*After some editorial discussion over the idea of putting our whole dialogue down here verbatim, I decided to keep this section intact so that my reader might have the chance of judging first hand what we lose by failing to communicate effectively with our most remote young people.*

-: so hows the book going miss rusty?

**Rusty:** its killing me.

-: how so?

**Rusty:** well you know how much you wrestle over writing articles. this is the T-rex of the article J-park for me.

-: yes i can imagine. you have got very far though. further than the fat guy. further than the black guy even. keep going.

**Rusty:** I could use a little help here.

-: Go on

**Rusty:** What is it that is particular about kids like you that makes you feel that school is not to be trusted? Help me put my finger on it. Coz the system does a lot to help other kinds of kids. I keep coming back to it being something to do with not giving your selves up. You know, keeping your pride when they want you broken to help you or something. But if u can, please help me nail it down?? Is it like the way some people think Asian people are alright if they don't wear 'funny clothes' and have too much of an aroma of spices?

-: What makes the teachers decide kids like me shouldn't be trusted?

**Rusty:** Like you. Like my boys. What is it that makes you fall against the hard edge of the system at school. And makes you feel the system is not to be trusted?

-: Emotional incompetencey

**Rusty:** Explain please

-: Teachers try at first to engage us. Then they try to connect to us. But we come from places where we don't really connect with anyone. So when a teacher tries to get on a level playing field and connect with a kid emotionally, gain his trust or friendship, it completely back fires. I hated having people try to connect with me on a friendly emotional level. Because I hated having to be invested in anyone's emotions or trust. Teachers try to connect with you by trying to display the idea that you can trust them enough to confide in them what your issues are. Every kid like me gets the sit down, serious, but laid back "come on, you tell me what's wrong" chat. But in my world that is just a sign of emotional weakness which can be exploited to distance yourself instead. The teacher thinks dropping his guard will make him more human to me. When really its hideous because you don't want them any closer. You grow up not having any level of emotional support at home so it's a scary and strange world to have it at school. I see it as a weakness, and because I'm afraid to be involved with a teacher or anyone else on any close level I use that weakness to hurt them and distance myself from them. Which seems evil to anyone else. But its safety for us. Its normal. If that makes any sense at all

**Rusty:** Go on

-: When you spend so much time secluded from and then running from emotional situations as a child. You begin to see them everywhere. You pick up on the slightest inkling of it on someone's face and then you act in a way that counters it. Or avoids it. Or use it to make that person look weak, which sounds terrible but it distances people from you. I don't think teachers understand how clever kids like me are at reading people and situations. When you grow up not talking, or sharing, or listening, or having emotionally invested, trusting, conversations, you have to learn to understand the world somehow. When you deprive yourself of all the normal investments like chatting with parents, being educated, connecting, you adapt to see the world some other way. You notice a lot that most people don't; like emotional weaknesses. And because this happens as a young kid it just becomes who you are before you realise or can change it. You're institutionalised into your own head before you know it. Some kids grow up intelligent enough to recognise and change or adapt it. Some kids don't have the abillity to figure that out so they become more lost. I feel like from a very early age i realised I was doing things differently. Which is a lonely thing to feel when you're young. And it perpetuates itself. We have no experience of anyone emotionally so we seek to distance ourselves. Through fear really. but you can't look afraid. So you get angry instead. You see the weaknesses in the teachers who try to reach out and you answer it with anger to get them away from trying to understand something you can't even explain. And the teachers hate you for it because its a totally different way of thinking and feeling. That they don't understand. Its complicated to explain..

**Rusty:** Please carry on. it's incredibly helpful.

-: On a good day though. You can feel confident and happy about things, feel like you fit a bit more and you come out a bit. I think that really gets to teachers.

**Rusty:** Why?

-: Cos they know you're in there. Somewhere.

**Rusty:** It's an astounding insight. Makes total sense. Can you help me out in any way with how I managed to become close to my kids? Given all that. What helped then. I wonder if in some ways its because I never sat down and asked maybe. Any ideas?

-: It only takes one tiny act of discipline from a teacher to ruin any chance of ever being closer, especially when they belittle you in front of everyone else like your shit isn't already hard, Just one tiny measure of it can switch you off that teacher for life. You didn't do that. You weren't seen as being that way because you smiled with kids. Not at them. Your smile helped you in more ways than you ever realised I think. It wasn't a false smile that we knew probably wouldnt be there later. It was genuine. news of it got around and kids expected it from you before they actually met you.

You didn't even realise it but we could see that that smile didn't mask anything. Kids who grow up like me learn to go by body language and to see right through people. Seeing through your smile only revealed a smile, and that was it. no resentment at being stuck with us. You didn't know it, but your smile opened up a lot of people to you before you even met them. It was constant. That was special.

**Rusty:** I'm reporting the world's biggest sniff here. Such a nice thing to say.

-: You didn't push kids to be anything. Or do anything. You pushed them to see why it was worth doing it instead. Which is intelligent. Which kids like me relate to. It's so important not to ever alienate a kid like me. Punish or alienate kids like me at school and its a life sentence for that teacher. I'd switch off from them. You didn't try too hard with kids to be anything you're not. Like I said earlier, we spot concealed weakness instantly and when we've spotted it in someone who's trying to lead us it's all worthless. You were never scary, mean, aggressive, or dictating. At least it was weakness that was there for all to see, weakness that we could secretly feel a bit safer in. Nothing hidden. No pretending. Or falsity.

**Rusty:** Wow. Listen to you go.

-: And your fit as fuck too innit. That always helped!

**Rusty:** I had just scrolled up to read your amazing deep analysis again and then I got down to the 'fit as fuck' bit at the bottom. It made me laugh. You're a rare treat aren't you.

-: I hope it helps

**Rusty:** It does. Immensely. I'd like to put the whole dialogue down as it stands. Its great.

-: do as you please with it. Its about as real its ever going to get. Its nice if it helps at all to clarify the situation with teachers and kids. Cos it is proper hard and proper lonely. And you grow to be such an animal when you could be such a good man. If you can do anything to combat that then you should.

**Rusty:** Thank you. You have more than made my day as ever. If you knew how what you say here fits with what I wrote in my paragraph about you at the beginning of the book it would make you smile. You've just done just what I said you do.

-: Which is what? What did you say that I do? How will I know when you're referring to me in the book?

**Rusty:** Oh you'll know. But by way of appreciation for your intel, I will tell you that the last sentence of your paragraph goes like this – 'That boy was an ebullient dangerous golden troublemaker who got in the way of progress in just about every lesson he ever bothered to attend, but on days like that when he put his faith in us and joined in, he taught us things about the world that we would never forget.'

-: That's lovely

**Rusty:** I'm gettin all emotional again now. Weak as ever see

-: It's lovely. Keep cracking on

*Sent from my BlackBerry® wireless device*

*\* \* \**

*I'm so glad I asked. It is easy to assume these kids lack our level of perception and analysis, because their communication and social behaviours operate in a parallel universe to our own.*

*Understanding Wild Youth requires accepting that you are a stranger in an alien culture about which you understand very little. There are opportunities for learning and finding common customs which can later be transferred from their sphere to ours. Like all journeys into alien cultures, much can be achieved with an open mind and an unshakeable belief that, whatever the details, cultures can integrate with mutual respect.*

*Many issues in the classroom come from a lack of simple courtesy and manners. A kid who cannot sit still, or wait their turn, is a major frustration, and yet this, and other problems can be overcome with an awareness that these skills are there, concealed.*

*English teachers are regularly demoralised by the failure of their students to recognise references and quotations from literary works, whilst the same students use film quotations and reference the mythological characters of X-Box games as a regular part of their interaction. They use humour and vulgarity to break emotional tension much as Shakespeare does, they value honour and loyalty to the home turf in Capulet and Montague proportions.*

*Once you gain an understanding of the sophisticated political analysis in hip hop, the etiquette surrounding the culture of skateparks, the smoking rituals of stoners, and the honour amongst thieves, your horizons broaden. We are often fighting a deficiency of regimen because we've failed to spot it, not because it is a deficiency. Find the true level, respect it, and it cross-pollinates. Put another way, people lose faith in a boss who doesn't recognise their skills and find ways to incorporate and enhance them for the good of the company.*

*One of the many things that gets me about Naughty Kids is how much they like to discuss their education. If they think their teachers are unfair, or the lesson is meaningless, they reject it. Similarly, if they don't respect the right of the person at the front to teach them anything, they reject it. In fact if they sense any hypocrisy at all from the direction of the whiteboard, they reject it. Give them half a chance and they'll tell you why.*

*For a long time now I have been forming the suspicion that these wild children have a huge potential for great things, and that they are in fact, our educational as well as our spiritual idealists. An embittered idealist is wearing to say the least. In the words of Joni Mitchell, they all 'meet the same fate someday, cynical and drunk, and boring someone in some dark cafe'. As a teacher, there is a duty to hold this off if possible, at least for the sake of the liver, if not for the sake of the someone.*

# Stop! Don't read this!
## Chapter 10

When you're the one writing the story, you see your characters a bit like miniature dolls' house sized creatures, that run around in the palm of your hand. The word 'creature' comes from 'creation'. It feels like it gives you a god-like power over what happens to them. Then you develop some sympathy with God (who doesn't even exist as far as I'm concerned), because once your characters are alive, you lose control over them. It's weird.

You think you're in charge of their tiny lives, and then they start to escape. They take leaps, build ladders, push each other off the edge, and before you know it, they've disappeared through your fingers like shiny drops of water.

You feel kind of helpless. Like they're vanishing under the furniture, and into the flower-beds. They could get killed by cats, or traffic, or the running feet of giants, and there's nothing you can do about it. So much for being the God of Creation. You just have to trust their safety in the hands of the world.

Truth is, the boys had got pretty sick of the whole Void Thing by this point. What had seemed like a powerful number for a while, their own version of being in control of the school universe, having an eye over it all with their web-cast of cameras, had lost its appeal for two main reasons.

Firstly, as I mentioned before, their final year in the social beehive of school was galloping towards its last breath, and the boys are livers of life, not spectator types. Their charm lies in being in the thick of it, not watching from the edges.

Secondly – sorry to state the obvious but, what is the point of surveillance around the building, when in reality, bigger events than school had ever seen – a drugs haul on a national news scale, and the horribly silent floating body of a mate guarding the treasure under the floor, had turned out to be more potential for movie-style adventure than anyone really wanted.

Be careful what you wish for.

Days had gone by. Everyone liked the idea of being handed a drugs' baron lifestyle and everyone had wanted to kill Billy at some time or another – but somehow no-one felt like trying a line of cocaine, and everyone badly wanted Billy alive and cheeky with his usual eye out for unguarded electronic equipment. Fantasies are awesome, but they have to stay fantasies to stay that way. The long awaited end of school approaching just made them want to be kids again, and the carefree fun and boredom of skiving and gyals and drinking in the park was a world they realised they loved as it slipped swiftly towards the end. ("What fucking cheese!!" I can almost hear Greg saying to all this). But you don't know what you've got till it's gone as some ass-hole once sang too many times towards the end of some rock ballad.

There was nothing more important than dealing with all that 'excitement' under the crumbling floorboards, but no-one brought it up, and the Void had become a place to dump your shit and get out into the light for the day. It had to be talked about sometime – but they kept on avoiding it until one day there was no avoiding it any more, and the underfloor nightmare forced itself to the surface.

It was a hot Friday lunchtime and the park was stomping. Smoked-out boozy seniors trying to ignore the squeaky shrieky juniors, and yet another argument between little neat, red-eyed Cleo and her forever bewildered-looking boyfriend. There was a delicious smell of half-charred steak from a disposable barbecue set up by Connor, a tall, mellow Year Ten with a pedigree for knowing how to skive in style.

Travis was lying shirtless next to Hamish in nothing but skimpy boxers, looking like gorgeous Mr Gay UK finalists, in an area of Britain where there is some pretty stiff competition, it has to be said! Jago sat nearby with music in his head.

Christie was teamed up with Conwell and Klit, working the crowd for some much-needed tobacco supplies: Klit already unsteady on his feet, but smiling like a kid at his family birthday party; Conwell's blue eyes glazed over as he focused internally on whatever it is Conwell thinks about.

Greg was lazily showing his power over wildly excited giggly girls, and Martin was sitting with his right-hand man, the cuddly bear himself – Pudgie Man, talking quietly in that half words, half telepathy way of theirs, sharing a secret joke or two as they do. It's like the world could end and after the smoke cleared, there they'd be, Martin and Pudge, sitting side by side in the ruins talking each other through what they'd just seen.

It was getting hotter and hotter. One of those breathless summer days you only seem to get these days when you should be in school, and you're secretly pleased when someone squirts a bottle of water over you, but you have to get up and smack 'em anyway – just coz you have to.

Then the world did end in a small-scale way, that is, they all sensed the end of lunchtime, and began to drag themselves back up the drive towards the hot, sticky classrooms.

Everyone was disappearing; Jago, un-gluing himself from the comforting shade of Travis, was one of the last juniors to leave.

It looked like peace for the seniors, until they too started to make tracks. Mitch made a move. Barney and Lewis were overtaking stragglers and bouncing off everything as they do. Even Hamish covered himself up, and Connor doused his barbecue reluctantly, The Chemical Brothers blasting in his ears for strength.

The last science modular exam was lying in wait for them in the gyms, quiet and dangerous like mustard gas, affecting Year Tens and Elevens alike, and sucking the sun out of everything. Soon everyone was gone and the boys, outsiders once more, were left without toys. They regrouped.

"Come on you lot, it's time for English!" boomed Travis, appearing rapidly with his seven mile strides like he does.

"Fuck that!" said Greg. "It's too hot for school".

"Yeah but we'll get our brews an some munch," Christie pointed out, always one for the positive side.

"Ma dad give me some money today. Why don't we just go into town? There's no-one around in school this aft anyway. Everyone's in that exam," Greg drawled on, that way he does when his mind is made up, "we can meet up with Rupert, he just texted me anyway".

They looked up towards school which was sweating like a teenager from every window and the decision was made. A smoke on the canal bank and a stroll to town. Looked like a plan.

"Who's got tobacco though?" No-one. "I think there's a bit in the Void," said Martin.

"Aw Noooo!" groaned Christie, "I've got to get that sixth form application for ma dad to sign. He's gonna kill me if I forget it again an I'm in enough shit wi' im already."

"Let's go to English!" Travis tried again, "Miss Rusty'll be offended if we don't show up."

"Too late," said Greg, "it's nearly two already."

"By the time we've fetched the tobacco we might as well wait for the school bus anyway," Martin pointed out, "save us a walk in the warm."

So it was sorted. Christie went off up to school for the tobacco and his forms, and the rest settled down in the shade to wait for his return and for three o' clock.

Christie set off at an enthusiastic run but soon gave up on that in the heat. By the time he was looking left and right outside the cleaners' cupboard, he was feeling the kind of tired you feel from sun and smoke and vodka with no money for mix. He lifted the trapdoor, flicked the power switch and stumped downstairs into the cool of the Void. He failed to notice a small tray which had been placed neatly at the foot of the steps with four cold teas and four smiling gingerbread men arranged round the sides.

He sat down heavily on the dusty old couch in HQ, reaching underneath it for the old corned beef tin in which they kept emergency supplies. He got as far as pulling out the small screwed up remains of a pack of Golden Virginia before lying back for a moment to enjoy a cool off. It took about two seconds for him to fall into a deep sleep.

Ah! The catnap! What a marvellous invention! His body relaxed in the unusual light draft coming through the open door, but not for long as he headed deep into a horrible dream…

He found himself in the place where he was, which is the worst place for a nightmare, it's harder to distance yourself from it when you wake up. It started with the now long-familiar rumble of change of lessons – like living under a railway bridge, you get used to it so you hardly hear the trains going over, even though the teacups rattle and the lights rock.

In the dream it seemed to Christie that it was a thunderstorm coming to break the heat of the day and he smiled a little and shifted in his sleep as the thunder died away and he heard the rustle of rain and waited for it to refresh his face.

When he felt nothing, he gradually realized, as you do in dreams, that it wasn't rain at all but something moving around in the furthest recess of the Void, something slithering or being dragged along the dusty floor. He felt like if only he didn't look at it, the slithering would go away and he fought the temptation for what seemed like an eternity as his skin prickled and the sound got closer and closer.

The scrape of larger and larger things being pushed out of its path made him desperate to open one eye just a fraction to see what it was. He fought it with all his might, like you do, starting to feel like he was going to make it. All went quiet for a breathless second and then the tiniest creak of the door moving right next to his head made him jump. He just had to see, and his eyes shot open. And then, as he looked, he felt horror creeping up his spine and shivering his neck as he found himself staring at Billy.

He had time to take in the shock of Billy's eyes staring back at him, frozen, and the filthy state of his clothes and the grime of his skin, before he was falling and falling, letting out one of those screams from dreams where no noise comes out, and everything went black.

Christie woke up, sitting bolt upright, his face milk-white and sweat pouring off him, only to find the rest of the boys standing in the doorway looking at him in surprise.

*It was about a year before Billy contacted me again. We had both been disappeared by that time. I had been in the national press for writing that line about flirting with him in chapter one. It was insane. He asked me for his copy of the book and he stayed up and read it all that night. I asked him what his mum thought about it all. Billy laughed, she thinks they're all fucking pathetic! Go on Billy's mum! I really couldn't have put it better.*

*Billy was permanently excluded, swiftly and quietly, and that was the end of five years of school. No goodbyes, no prom night, just a pair of trainers and some school pants in the drawer of my desk. All hail his unstoppable spirit for doing well in spite of it. Being excluded is a terrible thing. It's okay to do it if you are a horse-whisperer or something, but it's a devastating thing to do to people. When I was suspended I was forbidden to speak to anyone. This happens to teachers a lot I realize, but the conditions are so guantanamotastic they are just about impossible to recover from.*

*If you are a teacher, many of your friends are colleagues because they are the only people who can cope with you banging on about school all the time. If you live around the school community, a lot of the parents are your friends. Their kids play with your kids. What are you supposed to do? There's only so much going to the garden centre with your parents you can stand, and I walked ten pounds off my dog.*

*If you can't speak to anyone, you can't prepare a defence. If you've vanished, people start to think you must have done something really bad. If anyone complains on your behalf, The Powers look for new ways to justify what they are doing to you, and you can't fight it – because you can't speak. If you'd just killed someone and made bail, you would be allowed to talk to your mates at least, but not if you are a teacher who has contravened an internet policy which the school hasn't written yet. Hard times!*

# Stop! Don't read this!
## Chapter 11

"What the fuck happened to you?" demanded Greg. "We've bin waitin' for you for ages!"

It took Christie a minute to get a grip of himself before he muttered,

"Dunno, jus' fell asleep," he laughed nervously.

"Ere you'd better not have smoked everythin' without us!" said Greg with a hint of menace.

"Yeah you look like you've had a right whitey to me," added Martin.

Christie didn't say anything, he was still coming round, but he shoved the tobacco across the table by way of a reply and Greg, being the neatest roller, got to work. Smoking has changed a lot these days. It used to be like it didn't really matter what your rolling looked like, it was how well it smoked that counted. Now it's all about the look. Every single one you spin up has to be a work of art. I suppose it's a good thing, to take pride in your work. It's just got to matter, if you're going to take any pride in it.

Travis plonked the tea-tray they'd discovered on the way in down on the table like Exhibit 'A' in a courtroom and asked Christie if he knew anything about it. He obviously didn't, but he started straight in on a gingerbread man, biting its head off without a moment's hesitation and said,

"Nice one! These from Miss Rusty?" through a spray of crumbs.

"Must be," said Martin, "but they were down here, so if you dint bring em someone's been in here".

"Well there's one way to make sure who it was," said Greg, opening the laptop and taking a gingerbread victim for himself which he munched while he logged on.

He put in their password and opened the camera outside the cleaners' cupboard, rewinding slowly past themselves doing the left and right before disappearing behind the pillar, past Christie rubbing his eyes and slouching (but a way more natural Christie colour than he was now), until 13.31 where he stopped, zoomed in on the frame he'd been looking for, and turned the screen round for the rest of them to see.

They all smiled quite affectionately for a moment as they looked at the two familiar faces on the screen,

"Ah, Miss Rusty! Where does she get her info?" said Travis fondly as he looked at her [*er..that is ... me*] caught on camera coming out of the cupboard, peeping cautiously round the pillar with the usual Rusty Smile in place and a protective arm across Jago's shoulder.

"Shoulda known she'd be clued up on the whole thing," laughed Martin, "she's not gonna grass on us though is she? She never does. She just brought us the tea when we didn't show up for English an' left it like a message to let us know she knows."

But even as he was feeling relieved, a look at the faces of the others showed they were all thinking the same thing. Of course she indulged them over things that were a little law-less if understandable at street level, but there were secrets down here she'd have to expose to the light.

"Fuck!" some of them said, or all of them thought, as they stared at the computer and imagined how those two faces would change if they knew of the reality that the boys had been ignoring for too long.

How would either of them feel if they knew about Billy, sunk and dishonourably ignored, and enough drugs to fuel even a town like theirs through birthdays, Christmases and New Years for the next decade or so. The denial they'd been lost in opened like the roof coming off, and a bright chilling light exposing everything.

A heated debate broke out. What should they do? What had they been thinking? How had they done nothing except relocate the boxes? Gradually the shock gave way and they began to find some clarity. They might have to lose the haul of drugs to honour Billy as they should, but they'd been in enough tight corners before, all of them. There must be a way out.

The talking stopped again. They were stunned. Brought down to earth by their own inaction. They'd fucked up somehow. And still none of them really knew how it had been as long as it had. But life is strange like that, you think you know what's going on, and then somehow you lose your way for a while. It was time to fight their way back to the path, and preferably before three o'clock.

The silence lengthened – like everyone knew as soon as it ended they'd have to act. Christie stared at the table, Greg at the floor between his feet. Travis was looking at the screen, remembering the times he'd carried Jago on his shoulders. Martin was focused on the last gingerbread man on the tray, going soft in a pool of sloshed tea. He was trying not to see Billy, trying to find that place he goes to shut out reality and hear nothing, but it's been getting harder to do these days. He certainly heard what happened next anyway, they all did. There were sounds of movement, and harsh voices, and heavy footsteps approaching fast from the same recess as Christie's nightmare. Someone, quite a lot of someone, was in the Void, and they weren't school voices.

"Piggies?" hissed Greg. They listened again, everyone tensed up ready to do one, as the footsteps came to a halt over by the stairs. "Fuck it's worse than that, it's them! They've come back for their stash! We can't get to the stairs then. Fuckin' hide fast!"

Stealth escapes – their speciality – those boys can't half melt away when they have to, even a monster like Travis. Within seconds they were invisible, listening from various crafty cupboard corners to the irate sounds of the strangers as they discovered the removal of their cache. Their fury was understandable and dangerously real as they crashed around accusing each other, trying to establish what the hell had happened. Turning things over, kicking things around.

"Will someone tell me what the fuck is going on here!!" roared one voice over the others, the kind of voice that brought pirate movies to mind, that sounded like it was amplified by a pretty broad chest. There was muttering from the others as they spread out to search the Void. Travis, behind some loose planks at the back of a big wall storage unit, found himself thinking how differently these men explored the area to the way they had themselves. Like they had a right to be there. Like they didn't care who heard. It reminded him that nobody could hear from upstairs in the world. It gave all the boys a nasty uneasy feeling. It could only be a matter of time before someone was found. How much more was the world going to become dangerously real today?

And then one of them opened the door of HQ,

"What the … ?!" He called the others over in his strange southern accent and a hurried conference began.

Martin, roosting on the water pipes up above the table was the first to realise with a sinking feeling that the three men had found the laptop. As they gathered round it, he caught glimpses of them through the pipes.

The pirate-voice, probably the leader, or one that had definite leadership tendencies anyway, had a shaved head stuck on one of those Mafia necks, almost bigger than the head itself but no match for the shoulders.

"Rugby or wrestling maybe", thought sporty-Marty.

The southerner was of slightly skinnier build, though to be fair they all made Travis look like Bambi, and he had one of those noses that twisted and turned with a geography of bad breaks.

The third, he couldn't see clearly; an arm waved here and there, mousey hair, and a local accent which seemed to make his voice strangely familiar next to the other two. Every time he tried to get a good look Martin felt the side of his head scorching on the hot water pipe.

The way they treated the computer was like Neanderthals finding a time machine parked up in their cave. They prodded at the screen and the keys, but Greg's recent masterly application of a timed-out screen-freeze meant that everything they tried just brought up a window requesting a password. (Yes, people who are on the look out for security weaknesses always keep their own stuff well-guarded, and Greg was no exception.) Nose from the South was getting heated up again, cursing Information Technology. He was about to sweep the computer off the table when Pirate called him to order. They glared at each other and the Nose backed down.

"He's weaker," thought Martin, "but he's got a shorter fuse."

"We know who we're lookin' for. These two on the screen are the place to start an' we gotta find 'em quick. Let's hope we ain't too late," growled the Pirate. He lifted his chin towards Mouse-hair, "Go get the kid to keep watch down 'ere in case anyone comes back. We'll go sort these two out."

"I know where she is, I've seen her," said Mouse-hair shortly, as the other two took pictures of the screen with their mobiles, "that room by the theatre."

The Pirate gave Nose more orders as they looked again at the screen,

"You go towards that classroom, I'll go for the gate, either way we have to get em, and then we fuck em over till they talk. You carryin' yeah?"

There was a nod and a very unpleasant half-smile from Nose, and as they set off out the door of HQ, all the boys heard the loose metallic click of a safety catch being released on a hand gun. Sounds so seductive in a movie, just makes you feel sick close up. The gang made their way noisily back towards the recess till a distant trapdoor bang finished the scene like a full stop.

* * *

*There were a lot of questions asked at the disciplinary hearing about my motives for including myself in the story. What was the justification for setting myself up as 'the amazing teacher' etc. Much was made of the idea that I said 'Miss Rusty' would forgive the boys for misdemeanours and that this was a contravention of the teaching standards.*

*I didn't really go into the whole werewolf thing, given the line-up of stony-faced individuals who were putting a fair bit of effort into looking at me like I was some kind of monster. I tried to explain that I had to put myself in there really, if only to understand how it feels. When you accept yourself as a character, you are in some way exposed to the rest. Your actions and your personality are open to discussion. If I put the boys in that position, I might as well put myself there with them. A teacher shouldn't just sit there all secure and shove the kids out into no-man's land after all.*

*I think we had all had some prior experience anyway of what it is like to view yourself in the third person. The boys had been regarded as legendary rebels for years by that point. Travis once told me about the new headteacher's first day, when he got caught throwing a chair at someone (er ... Travis that is, not the new headteacher). The head shouted him by name, and they'd never even met. Trav was shocked at the extent to which his reputation preceded him.*

*My experience included my identical twin, Lola, who came to the school as a supply teacher for one term. I had a class of new Year Sevens three days a week for English, and one day a week for Foreign Language. I wasn't very good at Spanish to be fair and I needed the classroom more regimented than I like to have it for English. I told the group that my twin was teaching Spanish at school one day a week and that they should be careful as she was a lot stricter than I was. It's the beauty of new first years*

*A nation that is afraid to let its people judge the truth and falsehood in an open market is a nation that is afraid of its people.*

*John F. Kennedy*

*** 

*The year after the Commy Boys left school, on Friday the 16th January 2009, I received an email summoning me to a meeting on Monday morning at eight thirty. I was told to bring my union representative. I spent the weekend along with my friends and family wondering what the meeting could possibly be about. When I entered the Head's office I saw the book on his desk and had time to think – 'Oh it must be about that book!?' before being asked seven pre-prepared questions to which I was informed I must answer yes or no only. I was then suspended and told that that I must have the book removed from the internet within one hour and must not communicate in any way with anyone connected with the school or the media. No colleagues, no parents, no pupils no ex-pupils, no ex-parents and most emphatically no student named in the book. I was to communicate only through my union representative, Steve Cann. I was then escorted to my car. And I went home.*

*No teacher at our school had ever been suspended before and yet our school was a school like any other, it wasn't as if nothing ever happened.*

*An all-agency strategy meeting was held by the Head that afternoon in which it was noted that the Head would work 'vigorously and robustly' to distance the school from me. He provided the council's human resources, child-protection, legal and media representatives with a damning chapter by chapter report on the book which, despite never having had an opportunity to read it themselves, they agreed and logged as a good summary. It was also logged in this meeting that the parents were appalled and the staff were outraged, although there had been no communication with any parents about the book at that time, and no information was to be given to staff until the following morning. The complaint which caused my suspension* was made by a member of staff inside school and whoever it was that made the complaint has never been revealed.

It was suggested in the meeting that I might try to play the victim in this, or the whistleblower and it was agreed that the agencies should be proactive in preventing this. It was also pointed out that it would be in their interests for this to get into the press. When asked about contacting the boys themselves to see whether they had been harmed, the Head said he didn't want to drag them into it. To this day no-one from any of the agencies involved in this process has ever asked any of the boys if they were okay.

The following day the staff were read a statement which said that there had been a very serious breach of security and that no-one was permitted to speak of this matter outside school. It was not to be discussed with the students. I was not to be contacted. Some students were told I was sick, some were told that I'd gone to Russia. I began to receive texts and Facebook messages asking where I was and whether I was okay. I had to answer each one with, 'I'm sorry, I am not allowed to speak to you.'

By the end of the first week, letters had begun to arrive at the houses of named students from the book, inviting the parents to voice their concerns. The students learned why I had disappeared and sent me more messages. I could give no further reply. A demonstration was organised by the students and hundreds of them took to the school field in protest. Then another larger demonstration was organised. The police were called, the press were alerted and school ground to a halt. You-tube links and photos were sent to me along with messages of love and support. The Head enlisted the help of Steve to get the ringleaders into his office for a meeting after the protest and explained to them that this would make the situation worse for me. He said they should find more peaceful ways to express themselves. The next day's plan for further action was suspended and the students met *to discuss alternative strategies. They began a petition which was slow work as it kept getting confiscated. They set up a Facebook site 'Save Miss Rusty's Job' and began to air their views. There were several articles in the local press.*

*On the fourth of February I was summoned to a pre-disciplinary hearing. Here I was asked a new and longer list of pre-prepared questions which I tried to answer in spite of their lack of relevance. They were about why I had decided to publish this book, which of course I hadn't. It appeared on the internet on a print-on-demand website. It was at this meeting, which involved harsh questioning on the appropriateness of the book's content by someone who had previously called it a triumph, that I learned that the Head, with whom I had worked so closely, was now an adversary. I felt both afraid and bereft.*

*On the way home from this meeting I called Steve and told him that the Head was playing a double game and was not to be trusted. Steve was so shocked by this and the way that things were unfolding that he went home sick for the rest of the day. The Head called him at home and asked him to confide his feelings, saying he was worried about him and wanted to help. This was the only time in thirty-five years of teaching at the school that Steve had ever been called at home and talked to by the Head. He said he was fine, and returned to school the next day. He was summoned to the Head's office and told that a complaint had been made, from a parent who had read the publicity and come forward, and that Steve himself was to prepare for a pre-disciplinary meeting and bring his union representative. This presented some difficulties for Steve who had been the school's representative himself for years, but a regional advisor appeared to accompany him. It was at this meeting on Friday 13th of February that Steve was questioned about having the barbecue for the Commy Boys at his home, and for continuing a friendship with them after they left school. Steve pointed out that this was not news to the Head who had been informed by us the previous June and who had raised no objection. Now, seven months later, Steve was suspended for forming inappropriate relationships with ex-pupils of the school. It was never explained what was inappropriate about them.*

*Thus I gained a friend in my isolation, but now had no contact with school whatsoever and both Steve and I were on our own. The union provided us a couple of marvellous reps – Sue and Bev, totally decent and incredibly hard-working and honourable – but the terrain we were up against was beyond what decent folks could help with really. The Facebook site was expanded and parents and grandparents (some of whom had been taught by Steve back in the day) began to add their views along with the kids. We read it every evening. In our isolation it was like food.*

*On the 27th February I was in another pre-disciplinary meeting where I too was questioned about inappropriate relationships with my students. I asked why this all of a sudden when I had talked to the Head about it last year and it was no secret. The Head alleged that he had instructed Steve at that time not to have students at his house again. I asked him why he hadn't instructed me in the same way when I was clearly as much to blame. The Head replied, 'Because it wasn't your house!' When I asked why I was here then given that it still wasn't my house, no reply was forthcoming. Steve's insistence that he had never been given any instruction was borne out when the council had to disclose documents in the ensuing legal process.*

*The Head said he had received a number of emails which questioned his behaviour whilst championing mine. I didn't really know how I was meant to be blamed for that. At the end of the meeting I was told that there were very serious disciplinary issues to be dealt with. When I asked what they were, the reply was, 'I will have to think about that and you will hear from me in due course.' I went back into isolation while the media attention grew and tabloid reporters began to knock on my door. The suspension had an air of mystery around it.*

*The students, having been told to come up with more peaceful forms of protest, made badges, and got into trouble for wearing and distributing them. One of the boys I was being told I had harmed with my story was bundled into a police van at school for disturbing the peace with his box of badges. Some parents and former students set up a support group called Friends of Rusty and Steve and held a public meeting in the town. An announcement was made at the school telling the staff they were not to go into the town that evening.*

*The parents of the boys were summoned to school and asked a list of questions. Their answers were not included in the case, nor was the fact that they had come to school at all. When asked in the hearing why this information was withheld, the Head said he didn't think the parents understood the issues. Similarly, when asked what should be made of the many testimonials and letters from parents in my support, he said he would not give any weight to the opinions of people who were not professionals.*

*Several weeks later I received The Management Case with a list of six allegations, including Demeaning pupils and parents, Bringing the school into disrepute with pupils, parents, partner agencies and potentially more widely, Failure to observe confidentiality, Undermining the Headteacher and so on. It was eight weeks since I had been suspended and I was given a week to respond and provide evidence in my defence. My union rep succeeded in getting me access to my email account, and I found important emails had been deleted from it. The transcripts of the pre-disciplinary meetings were inaccurate and had been given to the Headteacher to amend as he saw fit. It is very difficult to prepare a case against such odds, and when you are not allowed to speak to anybody.*

*The Head's case was based on an analysis of the book's content as proving my failings as a teacher. For example, in the first chapter the boys leave the lesson nine minutes before the bell; this was said to be evidence of a disregard for health and safety. The case seemed to ignore completely the fact that the Head had approved the content in glowing terms the year before and had heartily encouraged me to continue with my book. The distinction was said to be that what was acceptable in school was not acceptable on the internet, whilst giving out printed copies of the book in the community with no restriction whatsoever had been previously described as a lovely gesture and was regarded as no breach of data protection or failure of professional standards at all.*

*I wondered if the Head had forgotten the emphatic encouragement he had written to me after reading the first five chapters the year before. I enclosed a photocopy of this note with my response to the case and awaited the summons to a disciplinary hearing. Steve had still heard nothing at all. Not a word.*

*In mid-April a local journalist with a remarkable turn for tabloidian reportage printed an article on the content of the book. It was headlined 'Miss Rusty's world of fantasy' and contained the summary which was to be repeated round the world in the ensuing months. I had seen this young journalist, in his slippery little fashion shoes negotiating his way up my path in the snow one morning but of course I was not at liberty to speak to him, so I had to let him write away without any reality check whatsoever. He took my photo from the back of the printed book and added it to the article, and the story sold. By the time it got to Fox News and some Brazilian papers the headlines had accelerated to, 'She wrote sex fantasies about her students and read them out in class!' It took almost five months for me to be released from the silence of my suspension so I was forced to sit still and watch the story roll.*

# Miss Rusty's world of fantasy...

*An extract from the first article on the content of the book*

A CONTROVERSIAL book published by a teacher refers to real pupils having sex fantasies about her. It also features a student "lazily" flirting with a teacher.

The fiction – Stop! Don't Read This! by Leonora Rustamova – is riddled with expletives, features pupils skipping school and drinking under age, hints at drug use and says the five main characters are known to police. The Courier has obtained a copy of the book, withdrawn from a self-publishing website when Miss Rustamova – Miss Rusty – was suspended.

Another teacher Steve Cann (believed to be a union representative) has also been suspended. The suspensions prompted hundreds of pupils to hold mass demonstrations and create internet pressure groups supporting the pair. They say the book was only written to encourage students to read.

It features five Year 11 pupils – all real students or ex-students and constantly referred to as Miss Rustamova's "favourites" – who discover a criminal drug den beneath the school. The story names several teachers, including the Head, and features pupils missing lessons, stealing phones and setting themselves on fire. One pupil is described as fantasising and flirting with Miss Rustamova, while she says she would do anything for a smile from another.

She writes: "It's getting harder and harder to see them just as kids."

Later she describes in the novel how the youngsters practise "orgasmic moans", which sound like "the soundtrack to teenage gay porn". One main character and a sixth student are described as sunbathing shirtless, "looking like gorgeous Mr Gay UK finalists in an area of Britain where there is some pretty stiff competition." The book ends with the boys being labelled heroes after revealing to police a drugs store beneath the school – although it is noted a case of cocaine goes missing before officers arrive.

"I suppose the boys had earned a hell of a ritzy summer holiday," says the book. Despite its shock content, campaigners say the book has helped pupils to learn. A parent of former pupils, said: "It's a work of fiction, even though some characters are based on real people. I don't think there's anything there that would concern parents, unless they're Mary Whitehouse types. It's no worse than TV shows like Skins, and just as fictional. I mean, drug dealers under the school isn't going to happen."

One named student, who has since left for college, said: "I can understand why parents might not be happy. But of the five main characters – me and my friends – all of us and our parents were fine with it. We like it. It helped us take school seriously."

The school, Miss Rustamova and the National Union of Teachers refused to comment because an investigation is under way.

Halifax Evening Courier
3rd April 2009

By the time the Disciplinary Hearing began towards the end of April, the pressure was immense. Still, I was curious to see how the Head would justify his initial positive comments on the back of the envelope which had contained the first five chapters. The subject came up in the first five minutes of his presentation to the governors' panel. It was asserted that in photocopying the envelope I had deliberately trimmed off a note of caution that he had written at the bottom about use of bad language. His word against mine. At the comfort break, I telephoned a friend of mine to go to my house, pick up the original envelope and deliver it to the hearing. When it was produced, the Head had to admit it had not been trimmed at all. There was no note of caution, contrary to his assertion. When a transcript of the hearing was provided, this part of the proceedings was obscured. Although it was acknowledged that the Head had given unqualified support for the first five chapters, had approved the final printed book before it went out to the community, and had no problem with the book's being read in class, the content remained as proof of my failing to meet the professional standards expected of a teacher.

In his summary, the Head stated that the book had been written in a shroud of secrecy to satisfy a fit of emotional need. He was ably advised and supported throughout by a member of Human Resources staff from the council and the Child Protection Co-ordinator, a woman who had neither read my evidence nor interviewed me on the matter but who was confident in giving a full psychological profile of my behaviour as comparable to that of a homosexual paedophile. I apparently suffer from 'Emotional Congruence' and this is clear from a reading of the book. Although she said 'there is no evidence of any sexual relationship here, and I hope I am right'... she didn't interview any of the Commy Boys to check.

Steve got much the same treatment after thirty-five years of devoted service to the school. At the time his employment *terminated, he also received his Long Service Award, along with a bunch of B and Q vouchers, and a Thank You card from the Head. I was branded with A Reckless Disregard for Confidentiality and Child Safeguarding Issues.*

*Our careers were at an end.*

*Both Steve and I were referred by the local authority to the Independent Safeguarding Authority, with a recommendation that we should be banned from working with children and vulnerable adults. We waited eleven months for the outcome of this investigation. No grounds were found for us to be banned, and our names were eventually cleared.*

*The day I was suspended, I don't think I realised the position I was in. I did what any self-respecting organism does under such circumstances and went into shock. I know this, because one little voice inside me was singing with joy at whatever mistake had somehow caused my boss to give me the whole of Monday off. It was a fine day and I made plans all the way home for how to make the most of this unexpected fiesta. I would pop into my friend James' office, drink some tea and joke about how the self-employed spend their time, then I'd take my dog into the woods, tidy the garden a bit maybe and read a book with my feet up on the hearth while the school bell rang far away every fifty minutes and someone sorted out this mess. Nothing worked out that way in the end of course. I got to James' place just after nine, sat down on a swivel chair, and remained staring into the middle distance till after three o'clock. People came and went around me, got on with work, made phone calls, and generally did whatever people do. And I just sat there in shock. Later it reminded me of a scene from the novel* All Quiet on The Western Front *where a young soldier runs on across No-man's land for a few more yards before he realises his feet have been shot off.*

*Over the next few days the shock wore off a bit and by the next Sunday night the pain had really settled in. I yearned for my school and felt suffocated in the silence. It's not the usual Sunday night feeling you get as a teacher I have to admit, but I experienced a rising sense of panic at the separation which was being effected. I couldn't understand why there was no offer to sit round a table and talk through the mistake, assess any damage and deal with it, before going back to lessons and getting on with the job. It was foolish of me of course. As the process unfolded I wised up.*

*I was saved that first Monday, by a call from my friend Naseem. She forced me to recall all the things I might have wished I was doing had I actually had to work. We went to the cinema at eleven in the morning and watched a Bollywood movie with large size lattes and a sack of Maltesers, had a good laugh, had a good cry and were home before three. That worked well as a survival technique even though Mondays were to get harder in the ensuing months. It atrophies the spirit to be workless on a Monday. Life is suspended while you are suspended and all you can do is wait for letters, the arrival of which you dread. There have been a lot of Mondays since then.*

*As the furore got going, the press, the protests, the endless interplay of acrimonious confidential documents, and the playing out of community reaction and debate, I felt motionless in the middle. I couldn't join in with any of it or go to any of the places I usually went to. I was in the eye of a storm.*

*The impact of an unexpected life-changing event is hard to describe. I had no idea what was coming till it hit me and then I was home and the damage was done. There were strange effects. I developed an irrational fear that when standing in the shower, the weight of the water being turned on might send me crashing through the floor of the bathroom. It actually terrified me for a while. I became nervous of traffic. I worried when my daughter went out of the door that she would never come back. How do people cope with sudden bereavement, or their houses being washed away in floods. I remember a boy once telling us about his father taking him to see Robbie Burns' grave. He described a statue of a fieldworker with a plough and a tiny mouse to be seen in the path of the blade. 'The best laid schemes o' mice an' men'. I felt mouse-like. Thankfully, it's getting harder to remember now how dark those times were, I feel like I've weathered the worst of it.*

*In August of 2009, Steve and I were escorted into the safely deserted building to collect our property. I had feared this moment for a long time, expecting to be overwhelmed by grief on returning to see my beloved school once more. I felt absolutely neutral. Turns out my memories of the school and the children, who helped me become a me to be proud of, are inside me, not the walls. The institutional walls are just that. Walls. It became clear to me that this is the effect of over-punishment, that I began by feeling so dreadfully sorry for the book's accidental appearance on the internet, and suffered such regret thinking that I might have caused my school and my Headteacher trouble. After experiencing first hand their attempts to have me crushed, humiliated and demonised for a simple technical mistake, I just didn't feel sorry any more. How is that punishment effective, which makes me feel like being an outlaw is the decent moral side?*

*The most successful forms of torture are those that use your own self against you, like the water torture of a drip drip-dripping on your head. I see more than my own example in the world where nameless foes choose to punish you for your own merits. I love kids, and I prioritised their value at school – it brought me brushes with The Dark Side more often than can be accommodated by a mere Star Wars complex. I have a lot of sympathy for parents too, and I don't like to see the way some teachers hide behind their position to make the parents feel like they have no right to an opinion on their child and its education. There are teachers who think the kids and their parents are there to get in the way of their career paths, and it is those people who like the idea of using an allegation like 'Demeaning Pupils and Parents' as a way to destroy the likes of me. They said I had fallen below professional standards in failing to establish fair, respectful and trusting relationships with students. They said my book was proof.*

*I read a dusty old tome of my dad's once about torturing spies in the war. The spies carried secret military information in code format and when they were caught they were tortured to give away the codes. You can't really blame anyone for giving in to torture – pain diminishes people so rapidly, but it was a bit of a problem for the military. Then some bright spark in the intelligence service hit on the idea of encoding the message into the carrier's favourite poem. Under torture you are far less likely to give away your favourite poem, because a poem you love is wrapped around parts of yourself you won't hand over to an enemy. And the more they hurt you, the less chance there is of you letting go of that. It's genius, and I hope the Bright Spark got pick of the buns at the intelligence service coffee break for coming up with that one, although I have to question the ethics of tying a person's favourite poem to such a dreadful experience forever. But that's wars for you – strap torpedoes to dolphins and train them to go and say hello to the nice big ship.*

*It helped me when they waved my book at me to tell me how dreadful I was. You have to hold on to the things which give you hope, because if you lose your hope and stay strong, you could end up like them.*

*I sat down at my old desk in the Ghetto to take stock of what was mine to take and what was mine to leave. I was pleased to see that the supply teacher who'd replaced me was at least as messy as I was. I opened the drawers and caught the friendly smell of pencil sharpenings and confiscated marker pens as I rummaged for my belongings. At the back of the bottom drawer I came across Billy's trainers.*

*I brought them home.*

*There are things that burn me now*
*Which turn golden when I am happy.*
*Do you see the mystery of our pain?*
*That we bear the poverty*
*And are able to sing and dream sweet things.*

*An African Elegy*

*Ben Okri*
*February 1990*

# Epilogue Reloaded

I'm adding a new epilogue to the one in the original, as it turned out not to be the end of the story. Far from it!

\* \* \*

*The boys completed school and went on, I'm delighted to say, to meaningful employment and further education. I started a new school year, with a greater understanding of kids on the edge, and kept in touch with the boys who I love, and who did me the honour of teaching me so much. I was complimented on this project, and a few months later I was promoted to a management role specifically dealing with marginalised students, whereupon (love that word) a booming voiced third-rower of the 'funny guy' variety in my year nine class said, "That's ace Miss! All us kids need is pied-piping by someone we believe in and we'll follow!" It was the kind of praise you never forget, but who ever forgets a bit of praise. I was ready for the challenge. The book lay dormant, as read books do, on a shelf here and there, and in the odd desk drawer and, as was later discovered, on an obscure website which was used to print it up. So I got sacked. ZWRyooP!!*

*Since then I have spent a lot more time with the boys, despite being deemed to have formed inappropriate relationships with them, and found guilty of putting them at risk. They've taken the piss about the way we've swapped roles now that I go to sign on, and they've told me to 'man up' when I get weepy about my shiftless life. A couple of them even spent the last year coming round to our house once a week after college to do extra English lessons. I still don't know whether they did it for themselves or they did it for me, but I like to think it's a bit of both. They treat my daughter like their kid sister and I'd trust them with the keys to anything, if I had anything.*

*I travelled to London with Greg and Martin to appear on a TV show. They hadn't been to the centre of the country before. We went on the train, chatting about the way things go, and were met by a chauffeur and a limo at Kings Cross. The driver didn't call me, he called Greg to say where he was waiting, and he stood by the open door holding a card with MR G Bratley written on it. Greg condescended to offer us a lift to the studio. The driver was so sweet to us. He liked the boys and slowed right up on Waterloo Bridge to point out famous sights for photos in the sunshine. Somewhere inside my happiness I was thinking about the many school trips to London which my boys were never on. I was so glad we'd got there.*

*At the studio, we were assigned a dressing room with our names on the door, and we laughed at what the disciplinary panel would have made of it, after all we would never have shared a dressing room if I hadn't been sacked. The boys were so touched by the way they were treated: talked to on a level by glamorous producers, and given articles of interest to read by the make-up ladies. On the show, the presenter read out the description of Martin from the first chapter of the book, and he beamed at her while he chatted away. It took me right back to the days when he was so remote, so solemn, and once more for old time's sake, it felt like my birthday to see his smile.*

*After two years of dutifully attending the jobcentre, and applying for endless posts, I finally got a job! For a whole month, working on the census, walking from door to door with a whopping great bag, following up on non-returned forms. The first six hour shift nearly killed me: feet dragging, aching shoulders, and wounded pride at my wasted education. On day two my supervisor rang me and said he needed to speak to me about an issue. When he hung up, panic set in. I was so sure that I was going to be sacked, shamed, run through the press, and undergo years of hearings. He met me later that afternoon and asked me to make sure I always put a code in the appropriate box when I issued a replacement questionnaire, then he gave me a cheery smile and departed. I was unrecognisable by day three. I had a spring in my step, I enjoyed the solitude and the experience of walking legitimately up romantic garden paths. It was that time of year when magnolia trees flower and all sorts of fragrant things go on in gardens. I got a feel for the details of my own quarter that I'd never had before, the mood of streets I'd only ever driven past, and I was jauntily putting codes in boxes when I issued questionnaires. I learned some cool new short cuts. On day four I got chased by a cow. By day five I had an epiphany.*

*I was thinking about that reaction I'd felt over the supervisor. I had seriously felt as if my world was about to crash down. It highlighted some major damage. I didn't have the slightest intention of writing a book about census forms and producing copies via a print-on-demand website, I took the job Forrest-Gump-seriously, and yet I was still expecting some unseen trouble to come out of nowhere those first couple of days. I mean, I'd been practically holding my wrists out for the cuffs. No cuffs came of course and in less than a week I loved the job as much as I'd loved teaching. I wouldn't have swapped it. Who you are carries over from one role to another as it does from one relationship to another and in a shifting world it's safer to be sure of who you are than what you are, to spot the damage as it tries to become you and lock it down as soon as you can with all the other bullshit that spoils an honest life. Well that was my epiphany anyway. I'm sticking to the mantra- Work like you don't need the money and love like you've never been hurt.*

*My friends were very encouraging when I shared these thoughts with them, suggesting that with my renewed positive attitude I might get another month's work in ten years time when the next census is due to be carried out. Dickheads.*

*A couple of months ago we went to see Trav's father: a huge old craggy Native American who somehow makes sense of the way Trav behaved at school. I mean if he'd been out wrestling mountain lions at break or something, he might have found it easier to sit still on those rickety little plastic school chairs. On the way back, Travis proposed that we all go out into the wilderness and make a squirrel stew. It's one of the problems I've found with being unemployed, that ready excuses like time and commitments are not easy to find when someone hits you with a plan like that. For the same reason, I find myself endlessly picking up lightly tanned relatives at obscene hours of the night from airports all over the North of England, but what can you do.*

*I won't go into the complexities of squirrel hunting, or the tenacity with which a newly deceased squirrel refuses to part with its fur, other than to say that my mother shows surprising determination when confronted with unusual domestic challenges, and we finally succeeded. We built a fire on the shore of a lake, and sat round it telling stories while the stew cooked. The stars came out, then the moon, and we horsed around at the lakeside. Squirrel stew tastes rather strange, although given that we prepared it by the light of an old wartime candle lantern my dad lent us for the occasion, perhaps I'm being a little hard on the poor old squirrels.*

*Later, I sat with Martin and Zoomo on an old jetty, swinging my legs and swatting at midges while he talked up our next mission – a roadtrip to the sea. Behind us I could hear the guys chatting and playing cards in the firelight, and along the shoreline, way off in the distance, I watched the flicker of the candle lantern bobbing along. Travis.*

*Watching his progress out there under the moon took me back to the start of the story. How defeated I'd felt by that group when they were hard-fronted strangers, and how unreachable they'd seemed, back in the day when opening the door to them was like lifting the lid of Pandora's Box. Sounds harsh I know when the Box contained all things evil that would plague mankind, but what the modern world ignores about the myth of Pandora, is its second lesson: that the other thing the box contained, was hope. These same boys have given me a lot of that. When they were in trouble they needed friendship, and when I was in trouble, they gave it back. I said at the start, that it helps me to see Time as a circle. In my first failed story-writing effort, the disastrous 'Woodland Massacre', I made Travis a squirrel, and here we were two years down the line, and I ended up making him a squirrel again. Couldn't have predicted that one. Well we couldn't have predicted any of it really.*

*It's taken me a while to come round from the experience of losing my career, and it hasn't exactly done wonders for my natural suspicion of happy endings. Even after being fully informed of how bad I am, I still don't feel bad. I don't even think I believe in badness any more. I'm not sure I ever did. The way I'm starting to see it now, I actually got saved not sacked, by five wild boys who weren't exactly everyone's idea of a blessing. Turns out that's exactly what they were. In a way they taught me more than I taught them, which is something we sometimes forget about the hassle of raising a generation. They reminded me that life is more complicated and more exciting than a system. And that there are some things the system can't contain. And that this is a failing of the system, not a failing of its teachers or its children, who should all have a valid chance that reflects where they come from, who they are and who they could be.*

*As a teacher I believe in giving hope, having faith, and offering children the keys to their world. I am not the only teacher who* has been punished for doing what they could to care for their kids. Sadly, there are some fearful narrow people in positions of power. They don't want the same things. At best they worry about people like us, because if people like us are right, then most of what they stand for is just made of paper. We of mettle become molten when we burn, while paper turns to ashes.

I quite like the revolutionary tone of that last sentence. It makes me realise how firmly I have chosen my side. You can't love a whole schoolful of teenagers and hate the possibility of revolution. Teenagers and revolutions are made of the same things: dreams, spirit, enthusiasm, feelings of oppression, a hunger for change, and a shit-load of testosterone.

# Acknowledgements

Given that I would be a medicated heap by now if it hadn't been for the incredible support I have been blessed with, my acknowledgements are set to turn out longer than the book. As it wouldn't have ever been a book without the people around me, so be it. I'm going for it.

My daughter Flora was thirteen when I was suspended. Her best friend Eddie had just relocated to Mexico and her father lived and worked abroad. Although there were many factors which contributed to my survival, it is Flora who helped me the most. There was an air of triumph the various times I was asked in the disciplinary process how I would have felt if my daughter had been written about in such a book. I found the question baffling, although I could see why they were pretty smug about it from their side, as if there was no room for regarding the book as anything other than a common enemy. I said I would have been concerned if she had got to the final year of school needing such an intervention, but the truth of the matter is that she wished she had been in it, so here she is.

"What are you doing home so early mother?"

"I got suspended for that book."

"Well you don't want to work for people like that do you? And you may as well go out in style. What's for dinner?"

Kids have such a way of seeing things simply. They don't taint issues of integrity with the kind of nonsense we are clouded by as adults. In the time it took me to work back to her initial reaction to the whole business, I watched my daughter transform. She took what was weak about the adult world and grew strong on it. And she took me with her. It was lovely being there to make her breakfast, and to welcome her home from school, even though for the first year I was often still up from a shiftless night of staring by the time she got up in the morning, and she came home regularly to find me red-eyed with nothing to cook on the days when I was too raw to face a shop. Flora had avoided supermarket shopping pretty much since she could talk. She hated it, but now she began to come with me again, keeping a watchful eye for the moments when I ground to a halt mid-aisle, and taking over imperceptibly to get us out of there fast. It's lucky she is partial to pasta and cheese. There were times when I got hysterical and was mean to anyone who came near me. Flora could slip past this, give me a hug and a steady look, and send me to my room to read a book.

On her fourteenth birthday, the story of my sex book for pupils hit our local paper. I felt sick all day till she came home. She said no-one had really mentioned it. Some time after that, up late again, I found a post on the Facebook live feed to Flora from some girl at school, 'How does it feel to have a mother whose a paedo?' I didn't know how to defend her. By the next morning when I logged back in to try to find a way of dealing with it, a string of comments had been added. Students from my school and Flora's, and good old Eddie in Mexico had all written explaining the reality of the situation beneath Flora's own response, 'I'm proud of my mum and her book is great.' There was no inflammation or mis-spelling or evidence of sloppy grammar. I am overwhelmed by gratitude to those children for the way they backed up my girl when my hands were tied. The empowerment young people get from their collective internet consciousness enhances and deepens their relationships beyond what we can really imagine. Flora didn't take the opportunity to become troublesome, she never even mentioned the hassle she got. She protected me when I should have been protecting her. Writing about Flora is hard. I can't even see the page for tears of pride. It's painful to watch the world grow your kids up at uncontrollable velocity. You can always see the baby in your own child.

When Eddie came home from Mexico for the holidays, our house was haunted by trauma. I was in one of my darker phases, staring into the middle distance and pretending to interact occasionally, having spent several days without sleep in the baggy old blue cardigan I wore religiously against all fashion and hygiene advice from my friends and family. When I finally went to bed, I discovered that the entire contents of the kitchen, literally everything but the kitchen sink had been carried past me and painstakingly re-installed in my bedroom in the original layout. It is the kind of tactic adopted by the Romanian secret police to unnerve people they are watching, or so a Romanian friend of mine informs me, and it works. The children found a humorous way to show me how checked out I was. By making a dream state out of reality they gave me a wake up call which reanimated the levels of domestic vigilance expected of a mother. It took hours to put it all back.

I began to return to myself, got back to regular sleep patterns, carefully removing the neatly pinned 'Don't even think about it!' notes from my blue cardigan before putting it on each morning. Flora, who never misses a day of school for anything, made an exception for the Employment Tribunal and when I lost she said,

"Come on, remember the Sex Pistols never won anything. It's time to burn the cardigan and publish your book."

This experience changed my daughter, grew her up fast. She became political, and her patience and loyalty have no edges. I wouldn't have wished any of this for us, well of course I wouldn't, and yet the friends we retained and the new friends we found refined our lives. We discovered a major positive characteristic in all those mediocre people who had somehow become part of our life over time. You know, the friends we all have with whom we have little in common, whose ideas and attitudes often appal or disappoint us, or worse still are just plain boring. When you are down on your luck, or to be more precise when you are suddenly a pervert in the papers, they all disappear, and they never come back. It is their saving grace. My marriage didn't make it either.

Spring comes and we feel pretty chipper Flora and I. People we love turn up at the door. We've learned to get by and be happy without money. We don't pretend to care any more about shit things. As the Russians say, poor people put everything they have on the table; rich people just put flowers on it. Eddie is still with us in two-dimensional skype format, although there's nothing two-dimensional about Ed. He returns to the UK in a couple of months and between them he and Flora have put together  a thirty-six page document to present to the Council of Mums for permission to go travelling together in the summer. It's a comprehensive argument- to say nothing of quoting Nostradamus or the Mayan Calendar or whatever in the list of reasons to be allowed to go- "the world is set to end in December 2012 so we may as well see some of it before it does." It shows they accept that apocalyptic things happen, and that they should be factored into life as advantageously as possible. I've caught up with them on that one. You can't stop life throwing things at you, and you can't stop life.

As to the monumental task of acknowledging people, I considered categorising them as friends, legal people, editors, colleagues, parents, journalists and so on, but as a huge believer in community cohesion I am moved by the realisation that all the categories seem to have merged. It doesn't help me at all with the practicalities of the thanking but it does wonders for sustaining my beliefs. My solicitor Dr Keith Lomax and my publishers Kev and Hetha Duffy for example, fit into all the above mentioned groups which surely merits a small cheer for the Global Village.

So thank you Keith for cutting through the Stalinist silence late one Sunday night, and taking on the howmanyleverarchfiles burden of being my solicitor. For the way the world cuts you deep, but not deep enough to ever stop you fighting for people who've lost the power to fight for themselves. For writing 'Stop! Don't read this either!', for your sympathy with human frailty and for your regular reminders that there are good people everywhere. Also to Julie, BLT, GLT and the Field Head Farm way of mixing respectability, decency, animals and anarchy in its truest form, with fabulous hospitality.

My publishers, The Bluemoose family. Thank you for giving me the pleasure of teaching your sons, and for being such true idealists not least when it comes to books. Kev for your dedicated tirades against capitalist notions of publishing and staying true to the integrity of the Moose. Hetha who just can't tire of doing things for those she loves. I won't forget the way you Duffys transmitted your friendship across the suspension and for your endless encouragement and support in everything that followed. The world needs more people like you.

Of course a huge thank you to my editors Hetha Duffy, Lin Webb, Michael Stewart, Gonzalo Garcès and Steve, the old school punctuation fascist. I promise you all I will make more of an effort with my apostrophes in the future. I thought I should spare you from having to correct all this as well.

My Urban Family. Steve, who has been the most tireless loyal friend: Hutch to my Starsky in our working days, fellow sufferer in the aftermath, sharer of hysterical laughter at two in the mornings when the funny side of it all somehow showed itself, and partner in general outrage on education, racism, classism, and the ilk. Jeeps for endlessly fixing the Lancia, making shepherds pie, passing his English exam in style, crying with me at Waterloo Road, taking care of Daniel Beaver, starting FORAS, fixing my laptop every five minutes, and being a rock for me and for Flora. Rosie and Paul not least for being funny when most needed and for keeping up the Star Wars paradigm, and Will for all those late evening cups of tea. Naseem for being the all time bezzer, holding me together across any distance, Ridley for being such a light, and Gav for his constant randomness.

My actual family and the Republic of Scammonden which made me who I am. My mum, who walked miles in the middle of the night to stop the press from finding the book on my doorstep (I had to pick something as an example, because there's no way of wording all my mother does for me), my dad for being all about books, my brother Saul for his constant faith and generosity. My godparents Rita and Colin who should have been safe to assume their job was done by the time I hit forty, and who have both been great.

The parents of my former school for giving me so much help, so much dinner, so many hugs in the street, so many lovely kids to teach and for writing so many letters. I was thinking recently how a lot of my new friends feel like old ones because they have their children's eyes. Some in particular I have to mention for their special contributions: Shaheen and Hanif for their friendship, and for obtaining me a burka to wear and go stealth when the school performed a piece I wrote for the National Music Festival heats. Thanks to Trish Merrington and those who formed The Friends of Rusty and Steve, the Save

Miss Rusty's Job Facebook page, and to Chris Ratcliffe for the Hebweb coverage. Those things helped so much in my isolation. Frances Tighe aka The Secret Grandmother, who taught me how to organise massive amounts of documents into a logical legal order. Caroline Duke and Trav's mum Wilma for being such proper mums about it all, Lesley Jones for cheering chats, and Janet Harwood for being a welcome friend.

Thank you to Matthew Pascal, a generous and honourable barrister and a great storyteller. Sorry you were so disappointed with the Commy Boys who ruined their literary reputation by behaving so well at the Tribunal.

To the memory of Lady Margaret Kagan, about the coolest woman I ever met, who gave me so much practical support, who got to the heart of matters so quickly, possessed such a fine humanitarian spirit and one hell of a wit.

These thanks go to all the kind strangers, members of the outer public who took the trouble to get involved. To Melvin Burgess for championing the cause so kindly and to Kate the Secret Friend and Constantina for all their legal support. Thanks to Trizia for her timely email which made me brave on a day when I was terrified, and to Johnnie Allen for his interpretation of the tabloids from a max security prison. Margaret and Bob Hardy for all their kindness, the many media people who helped me to clear my name and Ross Parry in particular. Also Chris Lockwood, my supervisor at the jobcentre who never gives up hope of me finding a job.

A special mention for my homey Kathleen Morton-Smith, my neighbour who I came to know from being at home so much, who sent me out on a horse when I needed it most, and who has become such a dear friend. And for John Gale who kept me to the fight and who doesn't know how lovely he is.

To my former colleagues who stuck by me in the disciplinary process, Sophie Grossova, Mark Middleton, Nicola Shaw, Andy Durrant, Ruth Roebuck and dear old Phil Ashworth.

I'm beginning to realize now that it is a dangerous game, trying to thank everyone who deserves it, like when school began to award a chocolate orange every Friday to a nominated member of the staff who had done something beyond the call. It was all warm and fuzzy for the first couple of weeks and then people started muttering darkly about un-oranged efforts they had made, till anyone who did get an orange felt like Judas Iscariot as they ran the gauntlet of applause in the morning meeting. Truth is the species would be nothing without the extra mile that everyone is going all the time, and trying to list the people who have got you where you are is impossible.

I had to ransack my house to find documents and evidence for the disciplinary process and all sorts of things turned up along the way. Amidst things like a note from a boy which said, 'Dear Miss Rusty sorry for being a twat today in English. Wont happen again! love Kyan', I found a letter from the couple who ran my primary school, a tiny countryside school, perched on the edge of a cliff, with about fifty pupils all told. They had written to me a year or so after I'd moved up to high school, on the occasion of my going into hospital – a get well soon letter written on a typewriter and yellowed with age. The headmaster Mr Wainscoat had added a post script at the bottom in fountain pen which said 'Don't forget we still expect you to become a writer Leonora.'

I hadn't seen this letter for years, much less remembered its existence, or their expectation, and it filled me with the memory of my earliest school days. I was an odd child (yes, surprising isn't it) and the Wainscoats gave me a little book which was kept in the top drawer of the Head's desk. I was allowed to leave the classroom and go to the teachers' study, sit in the old leather swivel chair amidst the smell of cherry pipe tobacco and write poems when the mood took me. I remembered a five page epic about a rabbit entitled 'Thumper died on Thursday'. It made me think about the seeds our teachers sow in us that grow whether we know it or not, so my last thank you – or even my first – goes to the memory of Mary and Arnold Wainscoat who were exceptional teachers and who first showed me that school is family.

*If all the world hated you, and believed you wicked, while your own conscience approved you, and absolved you from guilt, you would not be without friends.*

Jane Eyre
*Charlotte Brontë*